To the best of neighbors
Jerry Lewis E
7-10-82

BLACK GOLD
&
RED LIGHTS

"BOOM TOWN," a 45 x 45 inch oil on canvas by Thomas Hart Benton. This painting, located in the Memorial Art Gallery of the University of Rochester, Rochester, N.Y., is the artist's interpretation of Borger's main street.

BLACK GOLD & RED LIGHTS

Jerry Sinise

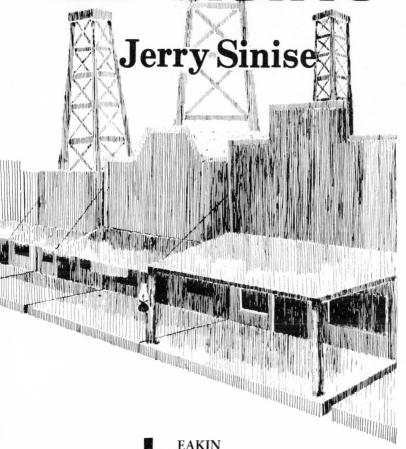

EAKIN PRESS

FIRST EDITION

Published in the United States of America
By Eakin Press, P.O. Drawer AG, Burnet, Texas 78611

ISBN 0-89015-338-8

DEDICATION

To my parents and brothers, Bob and Jack,
and their wives, Mylles and Lorraine.

We're goin' down to Borger tomorrow;
We're goin' down to work upon a well,
And when we get a way down in the limestone,
There's where the toolie catches hell.

CHORUS

She's a walkin'; she's a talkin';
Doggone, why don't you hear the linger
    of the old walkin' beam?
But the only time we ever were so happy
Was when we heard the boardin' house
    dinner bell.

We're goin' down to Borger tomorrow;
We're goin' down to get up a little steam
And when we get the gauges in the smokestack,
Then we'll see them walk another beam.

CHORUS

She's a walkin'; she's a talkin';
Doggone, why don't you hear the linger
    of the old walkin' beam?
But the only time we ever were so happy
Was when we heard the boardin' house
    dinner bell.

— C.C. McClelland
as told to M.C. Boatright,
September 9, 1952. University
of Texas Archives, Austin.

ACKNOWLEDGMENTS

My introduction to Borger came in 1945, when I took a bus from Enid, Oklahoma, to Amarillo, Texas. One of the stops was Borger, and I was admonished not to leave the bus station, because "this is one rough town." That appeared to be the prevailing attitude of many people during the late 1940s. Borger was a town to be shunned unless absolutely necessary. Apparently the memories of the Boom Days were still fresh on the minds of many who had lived and worked there or who had read about it or heard about it from those who had braved the dangers of the city during its earliest years.

During the 1950s, I worked for a firm making credit and insurance inspections and Borger was one of the towns I worked regularly. There was always an unbidden sense of foreboding when I knew I had to spend several hours in this town branded the Sodom of the Plains, worse, some believed, than ancient Sodom and Gomorrah of Biblical times, but I never found the people to be any different from people in other Panhandle towns and cities. I had heard of parents who would discipline their children with threats of sending them to "Booger Town" if they didn't straighten up. It had that kind of reputation.

While many bits and pieces have been written about Borger's Boom Days, I doubt that the entire story ever will be told. There were just too many things going on then for any one person to know everything that was happening. I interviewed several people over the years, but always came away feeling they really didn't know what had happened — or didn't want to know. Several people told me that "nothing bad" was going on in town, although they had "heard" that some tough criminals were "around." Others told me the best policy then — and now — was — and is — to "speak no evil, hear no evil, and see no evil." More than fifty years have gone by since those early, wild days, and some are still not talking about them.

What I have written is documented and comes from many sources. I am sure that in the future other books will be written about the town, and as a researcher, I hope there are. I'd like to know more about early Borger myself.

Many people spent many hours helping me accumulate material over the ten years or so I have been filling one file drawer, and they have my deepest appreciation.

Mrs. Pat H. Gammel, retired librarian, Adjutant General's Office, Camp Mabry, Austin, Texas, spent a considerable amount of her valuable time tracking down files for me, as did Warrant Officer Raymond Whitaker and Dorothy Ann Waldron, who helped beyond the call of duty.

A special thanks to Glenn Shirley, historian and author, Stillwater, Oklahoma, who allowed me to check through his extensive files; to Billy R. Ware, director, Bureau of Classification and Records, Texas Department of Corrections, Huntsville, Texas, for his generous assistance; to Bob Stephens, an authority on the Texas Rangers of old and an author in his own right, Dallas, Texas, for clearing up the record of Ranger M.T. Gonzaullas; to Sloan K. Childers, vice president-public relations, Phillips Petroleum Co., Bartlesville, Oklahoma, and Jack Heaney, public relations, Continental Oil Co., for their help in locating photos of early day Borger and Oklahoma oil wells; to Clara Kuehn, librarian, Panhandle-Plains Museum, Canyon, Texas, and to those at the Mary E. Bivins Memorial Library, Amarillo, Texas, and the Texas State Library and University of Texas Archives.

Jerry Sinise
Amarillo, Texas
April, 1982

CONTENTS

VIEW OF A Marland Lease in the Tonkawa Oil Field (Oklahoma). This field was discovered by E. W. Marland and the Marland Oil Company received a profit in excess of $25,000,000 from it. Marland built a hotel in Borger, Texas.

Photo courtesy of the Continental Oil Co., Houston, Texas.

PROLOGUE

The assassin waited. Thick bushes hid him from view from the street. He wasn't worried, however, about being seen. No one walked the side streets at night. Not if they valued their purses or their lives they didn't.

He checked his watch again, just as he had a dozen times before. 10:05 p.m. His grim smile thinned his somewhat full lips. His eyes remained cold, calculating. It wouldn't be long now. He gripped his pistol, checking the loads once again. This time he'd get the man for sure, bringing to memory an earlier, frustrating try. Not too long back he'd waited in the garage for the man. Had even broken out a pane of glass in the door to give himself a clear shot, but the man never showed. Tonight, though, was the night he settled it all — for all of them. The man deserved to die, he reasoned, and die he would! His probing, prying investigations were getting too close, and no one, not even a bigshot district attorney, was going to louse up a good thing. He chuckled humorlessly as it struck him that it was Friday the 13th. Lucky for me; unlucky for him.

He shifted his feet, moving his bulky body into a more comfortable position. He shook his arms to relax the growing tension. 10:10 p.m. He licked dry lips. A beer later. That's what he'd have. A beer later.

The September evening was warm, and the smell of sulfurous gas, stinking oil, and rotting garbage was thick enough to feel. Everything seemed greasy to the touch. A light wind carried the night sounds — the pop of opening beer bottles; the roar of escaping gas from near-by wells; the automatic honky tonk pianos grinding out the same tunes over and over in maddening monotony; the shrill laughter of heavily rouged dance hall girls and their not-quite-so-sober companions; and off in the distance, the piercing siren of an ambulance, a sound becoming more and more common in the growing, boom-ing town. The chug, chug, chug of steam-driven drills beat against him and echoed hollowly between the vacant houses. The noise never stops. Day and night; night and day. It's a 24-hour town.

A car drove into the long driveway, and its lights reflected briefly on the bushes. He didn't move until the auto was past. As it neared the single-car garage, it slowed, then stopped. Two women got out, talking softly. As they walked toward the back door of the one-story stucco house, the man drove the car into the garage. He came out, closed the doors, and started to turn toward the back gate.

The killer stood and pulled the trigger of his .38 calibre pistol five times.

The first bullet grazed the chest of the shocked victim above the heart and spun him around. The second entered his right side, passing through the third rib, emerging under his left arm. The third entered the back of his neck, passing through to come out in front of his right ear. A fourth bullet hit the garage wall and the fifth missed everything. As the bleeding man fell, he cried out, "My God . . . !"

The assassin pushed through the bushes and ran to the fallen man, checked to see that he was dead, then hurriedly searched through the man's inside suit coat pocket. The back door suddenly slammed open, and the women, running out of the house, screamed. The killer turned, ran across the backyard of an adjacent house, jumped a low fence and ran north down the alley. A door to an apartment opened as he ran past. A man looked out, then down the alley toward the sound of screaming and back again at the running man. The killer's face was in shadow, but the witness thought there was something familiar about him — the heavyset body, the awkward running — something he couldn't quite place.

The killer ran another block, jumped into a car, and sped off.

The first the town knew that something bad had happened was when the police whistle on top of city hall

HEADSTONE AT THE head of John A. Holmes' grave in the Panhandle, Texas cemetery. Note the misspelling of the words "assassinated" and "judicial."

began to blow with an urgency that cut through the other night sounds. It blew once, twice, three times. An ambulance's siren started up, adding to the sense of emergency. A crowd gathered in front of the police station, milling around, wanting to know what was happening.

City officials started arriving. Police moved in and out of the building hurriedly. Finally a policeman told the crowd, "Someone finally did it. Just like they said it'd happen. Johnny Holmes is dead!"

Also by the Author:

Pink Higgins, The Reluctant Gunfighter, And Other Tales of the Panhandle. Nortex Press, 1973.

George Washington Arrington, Civil War Spy, Texas Ranger, Sheriff and Rancher. Eakin Press, 1979

I

The Boom

It probably was happenstance that John A. Holmes was killed exactly one year from the day of his appointment as district attorney of the 84th Judicial District. His killer may have known that Holmes had been asked to fill the unexpired term of the previous DA, who resigned under pressure on September 13, 1928, but apparently the day had no special significance to the assassin. One thing we do know for sure is that it was rumored, no, positively said, that Holmes would never "serve out his term of office." Holmes was aware of the story, and while he gave credence to it, it didn't stop him from trying to clean up the city and county.

Holmes, *"A Fearless Martyr to Truth, Honor and Duty"* (inscribed on his tombstone), was born January 20, 1886, in Mississippi. His father, T.S. Holmes, was born in Durant, Mississippi, and his mother, Mary Ella Salus Holmes, was born in Salus, Mississippi. Holmes attended Mississippi A&M College, and the University of Texas Law School. He was at UT from 1907 to 1909, and while some indicate he was a Law School graduate, he was not listed among the seniors in the Law School's 1909-1910 directory. The only notation in the directory was that he was district attorney of the 31st Judicial District, Miami, Texas, Roberts County.

His address while attending UT was 200 West 17th Street, Bonham, Texas. Records of the Texas Supreme

JOHN A. HOLMES, District Attorney in Borger, was assassinated by a killer who waited for him one dark night.

GOV. DAN MOODY posted a reward for the capture and conviction of Holmes' killer or killers.

CLEM CALHOUN, flamboyant and tough, succeeded Holmes as District Attorney.

Court show he was licensed to practice in the 31st Judicial District on July 27, 1909, so it is quite likely he took the bar examination without ever graduating, not an uncommon practice in those days.

He apparently built a successful law practice in Miami, and in 1918, he was appointed district attorney upon the resignation of E.J. Pickens, who joined the army for service in World War I.

Holmes married Velma Green, and had one daughter. Mrs. Holmes taught music, and her mother worked for Locke Brothers in Miami.

When the big oil discovery was made in Hutchinson County in 1926, Holmes, who had run on the Democratic ticket for district attorney in the 31st Judicial District that same year (he won), resigned early in 1927 and moved to Borger to enter private law practice. Clifford Braley of Dallam County was appointed to fill the vacancy caused by Holmes' resignation.

When the Texas Legislature created the 84th Judicial District, Governor Dan Moody appointed Curtis Douglas, a brilliant young man, a University of Texas graduate, and the governor's classmate, to fill the DA's office. Moody, familiar with Douglas' habits, exacted a pledge from him that he would not drink liquor during his term of office. Douglas said he wouldn't, and that if he did take a drink, he would resign. As promises go, this one was about as good as most New Year's resolutions, and lasted about as long.

Douglas was ineffective as a defender of the people, spending too much time with a bottle of Scotch and not enough time prosecuting criminals.

It wasn't that Douglas didn't have the ability, it was just that he was easily swayed by the wrong people. Or as one observer put it: "The criminal ring laughed at the law."

C.S. Gardner, who was living in Wichita, Kansas, at the time of Holmes' death, wrote Governor Dan Moody that he moved to Borger "as a traveling salesman for the

3

Ranney-Davis Mercantile Co. in early '27. Soon after I arrived there I resigned.

"I saw what I thought was good prospects for a retail merchants association. That I organized — my first move was against check artists, but with not the best of results, as Curtis Douglas, then District Attorney, refused to prosecute. As it happened I officed with J. A. Holmes, who recommended to R. T. Macy, then Constable Precinct No. 2, that I be given a commission — that he did.

"I resided at the Marland Hotel, where your men [Texas Rangers] were located then. It was soon brought to attention that I was the stool pigeon for the Texas Rangers. That was not true — I did work many nights all night with Rangers C. O. Moore and Hale Kirby.

"When the notorious gambling hall of the Plains Hotel was raided by Kirby, Macy, Martin and Milligan [the owners] by chance were missed. The next day I placed Martin under arrest. The best charge I could get against him was a fine for gambling, of which he boasted was refunded to him. I was at once relieved of my commission and warned that I better leave.

"Thirty some Borger merchants petitioned Joe Ownbey [sheriff] that I be given a County Commission. It was but a few days that Ranger Kirby located the brewery of the Borger beer ring and asked me to help raid it. I do not recall how many thousand bottles of home brew we confiscated. The man we caught in charge turned over a complete set of books showing who owned, operated, and collected for all the different joints. We placed the owner in the city jail, and before daylight, this man was ordered to leave or threatened to be killed. He left Borger and we could not locate him. The owner of this joint or brewery was given a job as city policeman. A couple of nights later Kirby and I made the biggest catch of dope runners in the history of Borger, of which three of them were sent to the Federal Penitentiary. I was notified at once by Joe Ownbey that I resort strictly to check artists and such work and discontinue all other peace officer work."

Because Douglas wasn't doing his job, Governor Moody asked for his resignation. He refused, however, was finally forced to quit, and Holmes was asked to fill his unexpired term.

He and H.M. Hood headed the Democratic ticket in November and were elected to the offices of district attorney and county judge, respectively. He assumed office as DA on January 1, 1928, becoming, as W.D. Christopher of the Perryton Land Co., Perryton, Texas, wrote to Governor Moody, "a bold and fearless champion of law, order, and decency." Christopher, a close personal friend of Holmes, said that Holmes always stood for what he thought was right openly and boldly, "so that not even his enemies could call him a coward."

The conditions that brought about the assassination of Borger's district attorney were set in motion long before the town came into existence, going back to the discoverer of the Panhandle Field, Charles N. Gould, a University of Oklahoma geology professor.

During the summer months, Gould worked on federal surveys. In 1903, '04, and '05, he made studies of the Texas Panhandle water resources. Thirteen years later, when asked by M.C. Nobles, an Amarillo businessman, if he happened to know any place in the Panhandle where there might be oil, Gould recalled some of the big domes he'd seen along the Canadian River north of Amarillo.

All the geology he knew suggested the possibility of oil and gas, and he told Nobles and his partners in the newly-formed Amarillo Oil Company where to drill. They completed the first gas well in the Texas Panhandle on December 13, 1918, calling it the No. 1 Masterson. They then drilled other wells on the 70,000 acres the company leased on both sides of the Canadian, thirty miles north of Amarillo. Out of their next nine wells only one was

AN OIL WELL in the Texas Panhandle about 1925, a year prior to the Borger boom. *Photo courtesy of Phillips Petroleum Co.*

TYPICAL OILWELL IN Oklahoma during the early 1920s. This well was brought in by the Marland Oil Co., which merged with Continental Oil in 1929. Marland was quite active in Borger, Texas and built a hotel there.

Photo courtesy of the Continental Oil Co., Houston, Texas.

dry. The others averaged from six million to ten million cubic feet of gas per day.

Gould, also, was instrumental in helping to locate the first oil well in the Panhandle.

On March 25, 1919, Eugene S. Blasdel and P.H. Landergin leased twenty sections of the Captain S.B. Burnett 6666 Ranch in Carson and Hutchinson counties. They then employed Gould and his staff to survey the land. On July 5, 1919, Blasdel and Landergin and a new partner, W.H. Fuqua, assigned eight sections to the Gulf Production Company. Thirty days later, on August 5, Gulf spudded in a test well and began drilling on September 24, 1919, completing the well on August 4, 1920, at a depth of 2,411 feet. The well produced fifty million cubic feet of gas per day, making it the first gas well within a twenty-five mile radius of the Amarillo Oil Company's discovery.

Then, on November 20, 1920, Gulf began drilling its No. 2 Burnett, completing it on April 5, 1921, at a depth of 3,052 feet for an initial 175 barrels of oil a day, making it the first oil well in the Texas Panhandle.

The area developed slowly. For one thing, there was little demand for the quality of oil Gulf pumped; and secondly, there was no pipeline outlet as yet. Gulf, in 1923, drilled a 135-barrel oil producer on the Dial Ranch in Hutchinson County, and W.W. Silk completed a 215-barrel well, the No. 1 S.B. Burnett, in Carson County. Silk announced plans to put up a 55,000-barrel steel storage tank, also. Texas Company drilled its No. 1 Burnett in Carson County. And that pretty well told the drilling story in 1923.

At the end of 1924, there were sixteen producing wells in the Panhandle with a total production of 1,662 barrels daily, and by the end of 1925, there were fifty-six wells, bringing total production up to 5,536 barrels daily.

Two wells were credited with causing the Borger Boom.

On January 11, 1926, the Dixon Creek Oil and Refin-

PANTEX PLANT (now Phillips, Texas) looking northwest, Oct. 16, 1926. *Photo courtesy of Phillips Petroleum Co.*

8

ing Co., organized in 1919 by S.D. (Tex) McIlroy and his brother, White, brought in a well just east of what was to become Borger. Among the owners were M.C. Nobles, H.A. Nobles, Dr. M.W. Cunningham, and Mrs. Bertha McGregor.

Recalling the drilling of the Dixon Creek well, Fred Surratt of the Texas Company said:

> "Most of the first real development of the Panhandle Field was done by independent companies and 'wild cat' concerns, who in a large way are due credit for the real play. Very little was accomplished until the Dixon Creek Oil Co. brought in its big well, Smith No. 1, just east of present Borger. S.D. McIlroy, who had charge of the well, felt in very low spirits about it, being several times on the point of giving up, but because of his dogged determination, he stayed with the well. One day he told me he believed the well would make 150 barrels a day. The drilling stopped and produced about as estimated. It became necessary to go in and clean out the hole, which led to the suggestion that since they were in the well with tools, it might be a wise experiment to deepen the well. This was done, and the result was that the well broke loose and for over a year produced in excess of 5,000 barrels daily."

Some estimates were that the well actually produced 10,000 barrels daily. Five thousand or ten really was a moot point because of the excitement that discovery well caused. By October 1, 1926, there were 726 active wells and 600 more being drilled, and by the end of the year, 813 oil wells had been completed for a daily production of 167,597 barrels.

The second well, the one that made believers of any doubters that the field was for real, was the Holmes-

PANTEX CAMP (now Phillips, Texas) looking southwest, 1926.
Photo courtesy of Phillips Petroleum Co

PANTEX CAMP (now Phillips, Texas) looking north about 1926.
Photo courtesy of Phillips Petroleum Co.

Huey, a gusher that came in on March 6, 1926. Not only did it bring in a large amount of daily production, but it sparked a land rush that must have made Oklahoma's Cherokee Strip Run in 1893 look tame by comparison.

Oil and gas were the magnets that drew the law-abiding and lawless to the Texas Panhandle. Everyone wanted in on the bonanza strike. The visions of sudden wealth overcame common sense, and the discoveries provided a field day for the con artists, stock promoters, and land speculators. Among them were Lucas Miller, known widely as Luke the Spook, and his oil sniffing dog, Clyde.

Lucas, born during the witching hour on Halloween, October 30, 1900, thus the nickname, never did well in school, and, in fact, didn't do well out of school, either. His father, a hard-working, God-fearing man, did his best to thrash some responsibility into Luke, but all he ever got for his efforts was exercise and more rebellion.

By the time Luke was thirteen, he was incorrigible — smoking, drinking, and swearing like a mule skinner, and his father threw him out of the house. Luke apparently didn't mind. He moved into a deserted shack on a nearby creek and fished for his food. When the fish weren't biting, he'd steal chickens from the neighbors. Occasionally his mother would take him a pan of biscuits and a jar of preserves, and he would repay her by letting *her* chop some firewood for *him*. Luke brought new meaning to the word "worthless."

Time passed, and since no one would live with Luke the Spook except stray dogs, he had a whole pack of them in the shack and out of it. It wasn't long before he not only looked and smelled like his dogs, but acted like them, too. He did seem to have a special affinity for his mongrels and was able to teach them to do most everything — particularly steal. Luke and his dogs would enter town, and if the merchants didn't lock their doors fast enough, the pack would barge right in and practically sack the stores. Luke'd turn his dogs loose and they'd

11

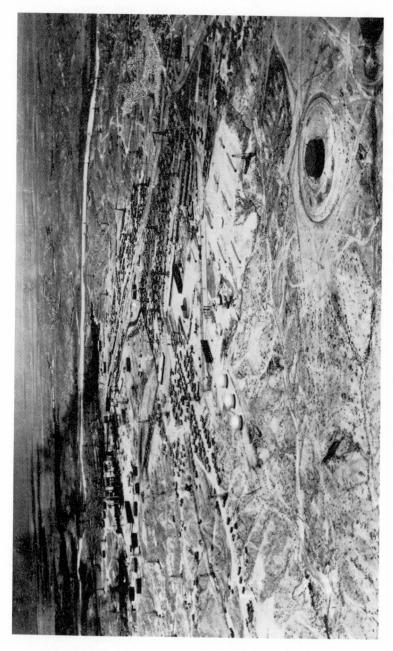

AERIAL VIEW OF the Borger Field, now Phillips, Texas, 1926.

Photo courtesy of Phillips Petroleum Co.

grab whatever was handy in their mouths and take off down the road. It wasn't long before the whole town would close down when Luke and his mongrels came to shop.

When the wildcatters poured into the area, Luke found a way to make the most of it. A braggart to begin with, Luke started telling some outrageous stories about the intelligence of his dogs, particularly Clyde. Clyde, he claimed, could tell if there was oil under the surface just by sniffing the ground. The snorts of derision and unbelief didn't faze Luke one bit.

One oil company decided to put Clyde to the test. If the mutt found oil, the company would pay Luke ten dollars. Off they went, Luke, Clyde, and several oil company officials to a company lease. Everyone stood on the edge of the lease while Clyde trotted aimlessly across the ground, sniffing. Suddenly he started running in circles, yelping loudly, and finally, howling to the blazing sun. Luke told them to drill where Clyde was sitting on his haunches. The driller did and hit oil!

Clyde's sensitive nose became a sensation, and Luke, always one to take advantage of his opportunities, raised the price from ten dollars to a hundred, then to a thousand. Money rolled in faster for Luke than it did for the wildcatters, and while Clyde's predictions weren't always true, they came through often enough to keep Luke in whiskey and chewing tobacco money.

Then one day Luke, who must have had around a hundred thousand dollars socked away following nearly nine months of Clyde's sniffing, bought a shave, haircut, bath, and a new suit of clothes — and left town, never to be seen again.

Some of the locals went to his shack and picked up Clyde. No sense in letting a good thing go to waste, they figured. They took him from place to place, but Clyde gave them nary a sniff. He'd just wander off looking for a shady spot and drop off to sleep. They were about to give up on him when one of the men took off his hat to

THE SWINGING PIPELINE bridge across a canyon near Borger, Texas, about 1927.

Photo courtesy of the Phillips Petroleum Co., Bartlesville, Okla.

ALAMO PLANT, purchased by Phillips Petroleum Co., 1927.

Photo courtesy of Phillips Petroleum Co

14

wipe the perspiration from his brow and Clyde went into his act, yelping and running in circles. The man put his hat back on and Clyde stopped, sat down and started howling. They tried Clyde out twice more and he responded instantly to the hat each time.

Worthless Luke the Spook had done it to them again.

With the increased oil and gas activity, a town became a necessity, and where there was land to sell and towns to be built, there was Asa (Ace) Phillip Borger, land speculator and town builder.

MAIN STREET OF Borger, 1920s. *Photo from Master Detective, May 1948.*

2

The Empire Builder

A cold wind whipped across the broken plains one February morning in 1926 when Ace Borger urged his horse up Antelope Peak, a cone-shaped mound high enough to use as a landmark. Off in the distance he saw an oil derrick, and it was then that he visualized his city of cities, the crowning glory of fifteen years of building towns where none had been before or rejuvenating towns about to die.

He had been living at 807 McGregor Street, Carthage, Missouri, when stories of the increased oil activity in Hutchinson County came to him. He had heard that some Alaskan prospectors were testing for oil in the Texas Panhandle, and if that were true, he knew there would be towns to build and money to make.

After he had checked out the stories personally, Ace bought 240 acres from rancher James F. Weatherly at $50 an acre, and secured a grant from Secretary of State Erma Grigsby MeHarg to form the Borger Townsite Company, with capital stock of $10,000 divided into 100 shares of $100 each. The company's stockholders were Ace Borger, C.C. Horton, and John R. Miller. Miller was an old friend from Ace's Oklahoma days of town building, and, as was to be seen, wasn't exactly a paragon of virtue and light.

ONE OF THE earliest photos of Borger, Texas, March 1926.

18

The company opened a townsite office on Monday, March 8, 1926, following a big advertising campaign in the Panhandle and Amarillo newspapers.

Your Opportunity Lies In Borger
The New Town of the Plains

their ad read, and for thirty per cent down, with the balance in ten equal payments, you could buy one of the newly laid out lots along Main Street, Johnson, McGee, or Dixon.

Before the sun set that day, the company grossed between $60,000 and $100,000, depending upon the report you read. By the end of six months, the company grossed more than $1 million on its $12,000 investment.

Ace also knew what was going to happen to the town. He'd been down this road several times before in Oklahoma. Once he started selling his 25 by 120 feet lots at $1,500 each, the town's population went from zero to 15,000 within a couple of months, and at its peak, there may have been 25,000 to 30,000 people in town. The sudden influx, resulting from the oil discoveries, provided a made-to-order situation for graft, theft, and other forms of corruption, none of which seemed to bother Ace and his partners one bit.

Ace made his living from selling real estate and lumber, both profitable ventures as expected. Town building, he had found, was, when properly managed, lucrative. He started selling real estate in 1919, successfully promoting homesites in Picher, Cromwell, and Slick, all in Oklahoma. He became the guiding genius who took dying towns and brought them back to life, and if, as a result of his efforts, the towns became more lively than some of their citizens desired, so be it.

Ace brought new meaning to the term "wide open." Cromwell, a case in point, was so wide open it was regarded as "the most wicked city in the world." But then, Borger as a town hadn't been built yet.

19

BORGER, TEXAS, 90 days old. This is Main Street looking south.
Photo courtesy Phillips Petroleum Company

Borger, at first, was a city of strangers migrating from every section of the nation to the Texas Plains for one reason — to cash in on the sudden wealth. It was a city in constant flux and that in itself left it vulnerable to the Machiavellian machinations of its rulers, who took advantage of the fact that people didn't know each other, thereby gaining the confidence of enough of the citizens to swing an election.

On October 28, 1926, the city was incorporated and the man who wanted to be mayor, John R. Miller, got his wish. Miller, an attorney by vocation, had a somewhat shady past in Oklahoma, and it seemed that wherever Borger started a town, Miller was there too. Miller brought into town his close friend, Two Gun Dick Herwig, an indicted murderer and sadistic enforcer, to bolster the city's law. Miller also induced Ma and Pa Murphy to leave Cromwell and set up their dance hall and string of girls in Borger. None of these additions to Borger's society would make the social register.

Miller, said by some to be the "king of Borger and president of the whiskey line," had a winning way with the "wild women, bootleggers, and gamblers," and was deeply involved in payoffs from each of these underworld groups.

Pa Murphy, a gross, fat, heavy-jowled, wide-shouldered, former fighter, represented all that was bad in the booming city, and his wife was just as notorious.

In his book, *Borger, the Little Oklahoma,* oil driller John P. (Slim) Jones told this interesting story about the fig leaf dance at Pop Murphy's dance hall:

> I heard about the dance that Pop Murphy was going to have known as the "Fig Leaf Dance." Pop was an old friend of Miller, who gave him permission to have it. I decided to go as I understood there would be no clothes on. Just a few fig leaves over a small portion of the body. I went early so I wouldn't miss anything

EARLY DAY STREET scene, Borger, Texas, 1926.

Photo courtesy of the Hutchinson County Historical Commission.

and I didn't. Owing to the short summer in the Panhandle and the cold winters, there were no fig trees so they decided to have the dance anyway and I didn't miss seeing anything but the fig leaves. The house was unusually crowded. I didn't dance myself, but it was no trouble for the girls to get partners and the longer they danced the rougher they got. Someone called the chief of police and he made an attempt to break it up. He was told that Pop Murphy had permission from the mayor. Anyway, the chief overruled the mayor's decision and broke it up. I hope reading this won't encourage anyone to start the dance again. If they do, I hope it will be in fig country where fig leaves are plentiful.

Of all the entertainment places in town, the dance halls were the most popular, and Murphy's place seemed to head the list. Murphy'd stand behind a short counter and call out the dances, with each one lasting about two minutes. At the end of each, Murphy would bellow, "Bring 'er in!" The girls would lead their partners to the counter and Murphy would collect twenty-five cents. The girls' share was ten cents. Then Murphy would yell, "Turn 'er over, boys," and the music, from a three to five piece band, would start again.

Ma Murphy, one tough lady, kept a tight control on her girls, but saw to it they solicited actively in and out of the dance hall. She was jailed eventually in Kansas City on white slavery charges.

To talk to Pop Murphy, however, you'd think he and his wife were running a proper business and all and that the town's reputation wasn't what outsiders said it was. Edward B. Garnett, Sunday editor of *The Kansas City Star,* interviewed Murphy in 1927, and quoted the dance hall owner as saying,

"Get me right, boys, Borger is not a bad town. There are no bad men here — no, nor bad women, either. My girls are all decent. If they ain't they don't work in my dance hall. If a girl dances in my place, she must dance. No sitting 'em out or sneaking away between dances. If she sneaks out — well, she's out, that's all. And she don't come back — not to Murphy's.

"Now as for the bad men, let me tell you how that is. One night just after the Rangers came over here to see that everything got along in good order, a young feller goes into one of the soft drink places with some hardware. No more than gets inside the front door till one of the Rangers steps up to meet him.

"Says the Ranger: 'Why, sonny, what's the trouble? What you got them revolvers for? You mustn't be carrying fire-arms around town. Tut, tut, young man, put 'em down. Gosh, they might be loaded and go off and hurt somebody.' And he just carelessly put an arm across that kid's shoulder, the guns came down and was delivered over to the Ranger, and out he goes with the kid, arm in arm, just like two brothers. That's the kind of bad men we have. People have tried to make us out as a hell-raisin' town. It's movie stuff, I'd say."

"But why did Rangers come?" asked Garnett.

"Oh, they ain't been here long and are clearin' out tomorrow — maybe tonight." Was there a flicker of hope among the bystanders? "Both of them are swell guys and regular fellers."

Both of them?" Garnett asked, slightly surprised. "Are there only two?"

"Sure — two's enough. Borger ain't a bad town."

This, then, is the town that Ace built.

Saloons, such as the Bloody Bucket, Green Parrot, Bevo Mill, Palisades, Rattlesnake Inn, to name a few, were notorious for their poor whiskey and willing girls. Houses of ill repute abounded, and as a result, venereal disease reached epidemic proportions in Borger.

One oilfield worker recalled his stay in a bunkhouse owned by the Phillips Petroleum Co.:

> There were fifty-five men in this bunkhouse. You slept on cots ... and at the time, there were eighteen men that had VD in that department ... Just over the hill on the Mary Huck lease, they had a bunkhouse and of the fourteen boys examined, nine had VD.

Borger pedestrians sometimes were exhorted to take a pamphlet given out by a young man on a Main Street corner:

> Over three hundred diseases of men with remedies given are listed in this wonderful little book, gentlemen. Venereal diseases given special attention. It's a cheap bargain at two dollars. It's dirt cheap at one dollar. But I'm selling it at the unheard of price of fifty cents. Who wants one, gentlemen?

There were gaming halls, dope peddling, illegal whiskey, slot machines, and most any other forms of corruption imaginable. Payoffs to city officials were common — and expected. The open card gambling houses created a problem for the oil companies, and company officials finally had to lay down the law to their employees concerning them. The companies wanted them closed because "workers refused to stay on the job as long as they could sit in on a poker, red dog, or blackjack game. With the dives and joints running full blast in 'domino halls' and in the rear of rooming houses, drink stands, and elsewhere, the officials said they could not maintain sufficient forces to do necessary work."

Poker, blackjack, and other card games were held nightly, but most were "private" games. Another way to lose one's money was in the carnival stands on the streets of Borger. There were numerous places one could take a "shot at the nigger dolls" for twenty-five cents for three balls. The coin was placed on a marked square indicating whether one bets he will knock the dolls over or off their pedestals. If the dolls go over or off, even money is paid. Lead loads in the dolls made them hard to knock over and impossible to knock off.

Prostitution was big business in Borger, not only for the "Borger Belles," but for police, sheriff department officials, pimps, and some of the higher-ups in city hall. Herwig's job, in addition to that of enforcer, was to collect $18 per week from each of these women, and if they didn't payoff, they were slapped around, threatened with broken arms and faces. They paid, and estimates are that more than $500,000 was collected within a six-month period from the girls.

In describing them, a newspaperman said they were "gaudily dressed, with abbreviated skirts ending with hose tops, mixing frippery with coarse talk. Their young faces were highly decorated with livid rouge, eyes ringed with a pale grey, and topped with arched and greased eyebrows. Lashes were beaded with mascara, and experienced painted lips emitted endless rings of cigarette smoke."

Although John P. (Slim) Jones in Volume II of *Borger, The Little Oklahoma,* says "this is a true story of a girl, a white girl, a wise girl who was raised in Kansas City, Missouri," it is more than likely the tale of the Queen of Dickson [*sic*] Street is apocryphal. No documentation could be found that it ever happened, but Jones provides some insight into some of the things that could have gone on behind the scenes in Borger, and for that reason it is included in this book.

It is a story of a sister and brother, no names given. Their father died when she was sixteen and he was twenty-one. Three months later, their mother died. Although both sister and brother were well educated, he had no special work and turned to gambling and "having a good time." When the inheritance was gone, he began stealing and hijacking. An outlaw friend suggested the young man move to Borger and see a man there known as Kansas City Jack.

He told his sister he was moving, and she insisted on going with him. When they got to Borger, he placed her in a shack in the Whittenburg townsite, and he started looking for Kansas City Jack. On the way, he met Mary, a prostitute he had known in his hometown. Through her, he met Jack, reportedly one of Borger's real bad men — gambler, thief, killer.

The young man went to work for him, but found his pay was not high enough, and he branched off on his own, becoming a hired gun. Jones says his job "was to kill any man or woman who was pointed out to him by the gang of the underworld."

Then, he began pimping for three to four women, and started making something of a reputation for himself. He was called the Kansas City Kid, because of his age.

His sister became restless, and although he tried to keep her pure and innocent, she wanted to have a good time. "She lacked a moral sense," Jones says. So she went out alone, waking up one night in a cheap hotel on Main Street. She had been in one of Borger's dance halls, had allowed two men to buy her drinks, and ended up losing her virginity, although that did not seem to bother her. She did resolve, however, that she would not allow others to use her without paying well for it.

She told her brother, and, with a shrug, he thought he would add her to his string of girls. She did not want that, but wanted him to introduce her to "some of the wealthy gamblers and bootleggers." She soon became a well recognized figure at wrestling matches, prize fights, and "the more sparkling dances of the underworld."

The teen-ager became the mistress of the "King of the Bootleggers of Northwest Texas." One night, however, he slapped her around and she defended herself with an automobile crank, thus ending that particular association.

Some of her friends, she learned, were opium users, and she allowed one of them to take her to a small Chinese restaurant on Dickson [*sic*] Street. "She engaged the Chinese men in conversation and indicated that she was willing to be intimate with them for a price, an invitation into the pleasures of opium."

She became the lover of one of the wealthiest of the Chinese, and he established her in a "room elaborate with silk and satin."

Her brother wanted her home, but she refused. He then sent word he would come and get her if she did not come of her own accord. The Chinaman moved her to another location; however, her brother found her again and sent a threatening letter, warning "that he would bring down his whole gang of men if the girl did not return."

"Your brother is not wise," the girl's lover said.

"He has got to leave me alone," the girl said.

The Chinaman made arrangements to protect the girl by hiring some gunmen to be near when the girl, brother, and Chinaman met to talk it over.

"You've got to come home," the brother told his sister.

She refused.

He towered over her. "I will make you come!"

The Chinaman interferred. "You speak to my wife like that?" They weren't married, but that was a moot point.

The brother grabbed the girl's arm, but she pulled

A $175,000 FIRE in Borger, Dec. 8, 1926. The buildings were rebuilt in less than 60 days.

Photo courtesy of the Hutchinson County Historical Commission.

away and hid behind her lover. The brother pushed the Chinaman aside and grabbed the girl. The Chinaman pulled out a small pearl handled revolver. "I'll fix him," he said.

She stared at her brother, then nodded. The Chinaman lifted his head and four gunmen came out from hiding. They held his arms. The youth's sister looked at him as if he were a stranger. "Get rid of him. I won't have him bothering me."

A knife flashed and her brother was dead.

After that the Queen of Dickson [sic] Street came into her own. She wore silks and jewels. One day, however, the Chinaman came to her and said, "My wife is not happy. She says I think more of you than I do of her. I must quit you and get another ordinary girl, not a queen." He suggested another man who wanted a mistress. Since he was wealthy, she did not care.

Then she had a succession of lovers, living well for six months in one lavish apartment after another. One man tried to get her to give up her wandering life and live exclusively with him. Some said he was one of Borger's wealthiest men. He offered her anything she wanted. The girl sneered at him. He finally convinced her to try his life for a while, and they went to the most expensive places, drank the best gin, ate the best food. The girl, Slim Jones says, "saw what a gold mine he might prove to be." He would ask her if she were ready to leave the tawdry life she was living to be with him.

The girl said later that "he had too much sense to talk about marriage and make an honest woman of me. He was a clean sport all right. He had me going half a dozen times. There was nothing he could not have bought me, but then, I would think of the boys down on Dickson Street and I wasn't sure. It was the dope I was thinking about."

Leave Dickson Street? That she couldn't do.

Then a young preacher called on her "as part of his Christian duty," and fell madly in love with her. He pleaded with her to leave her life of sin. She wouldn't. At last her patience wore thin, and she said, "That isn't what you want me to do."

He insisted that it was.

Jones says she then "leaned on her couch deliberately displaying more of her charms than he had yet seen. "Isn't it me you are really interested in?"

"Why . . . why . . . ," the very idea made him tongue tied. "Of course, I'm interested in you as a possible convert."

Then she sat up. "If I agree to become a Christian and join some church on condition that you never see me again is that what you want?"

"No, I don't want you to do that."

She looked him straight in the eye. "No, you're just like the rest. You want my body, not my soul."

"I want your soul," he insisted.

"My soul belongs to the Devil, but my body belongs to me," she said.

The girl then tempted him beyond anything he had experienced ever before, offering herself to him. She teased him, moving close to him, and when he went to put his arms around her, she moved quickly away.

"You're just like the rest. You betray your God for a woman's body, and you haven't the manhood to say what you want," she sneered.

Shamed, the young preacher stumbled out of the room.

A few days later they found him dead in a cheap hotel room — a suicide.

The girl plunged even deeper and more wildly into her life of dissipation. Her beauty began to wane, her clothing becoming shoddy. She was forced to move out of the nicer rooms in town to a shack she shared with a cheap gambler. He was killed.

"Her figure became angular and her face hard and lined. People no longer spoke of her as the Queen of Dickson Street." She finally started coming to her

31

senses and began to take care of herself. A man she had known in Kansas City proposed marriage and she accepted. Two days prior to the marriage, however, she turned to a final fling with opium. She sold herself to pay for it. It was one pipe after another until she lapsed into unconsciousness. Her husband-to-be found her in a shack on the day of their wedding.

Jones says, "A doctor was summoned and at once pronounced the case pnuemonia. Her body, ravaged by years of dissipation, could not resist the attack of the germs. Within a week she was dead. Dickson Street did not mourn her passing for as a queen, she had passed long ago."

"Prohibition," an author wrote, "was the longest, craziest, funniest, bloodiest adventure in reform in American history—thirteen years, ten months, and eighteen days of hedonistic purgatory for America's great drinking class."

When Ace built his town, this futile attempt to regulate the morals of the nation's citizens was six years old. Prohibition began at 12:01 a.m. on January 16, 1920, when the Eighteenth Amendment took effect, proclaiming that the very large portion of 122 million Americans, who had been accustomed to drinking some two billion gallons of alcoholic beverages yearly, must henceforth cease and desist.

Bootlegging, as prostitution, was the second, if not the first, biggest business in the city of Borger, and mixed with the stink of pumping oil was the smell of sour mash from the hidden stills spotted throughout the hills and rocky canyons.

King of the bootleggers was Johnny Waltine Popejoy, known throughout the territory as "Shine," short for moonshine. He was meaner than a junkyard dog. His brother, Torrance (Jet), wasn't much better.

Shine was born in 1885 in the Ozark hills of Arkansas, but grew up around Henryetta, Oklahoma, a part of the world which spawned more than its share of outlaws. As a teen-ager he turned to gambling, bootlegging, and moonshining, and he celebrated his twenty-first birthday by holding up the Henryetta Post Office. He was captured three hours later. He stood trial but was released when the postmaster, who could identify him, vanished.

Shine was about as coldblooded as anyone could get. During his days in Oklahoma, he had an old man help him operating his stills. It seems the old man came down with a hacking cough and became so weak he could hardly get around. The doctor diagnosed it as tuberculosis and told the old man he had only a few weeks to live. The man went to Shine, told him his problems and asked to be put out of his misery. Since he had no money for a burial plot, he asked to be buried in the woods behind Shine's house. Shine gave him money for a coffin and let him dig his own grave. When the old man had finished, Shine shot him and buried him.

The new city of Borger was ideal for his talents, but he ran into too rough a crowd to compete in town, so he opened a place called The Rooming House in nearby Signal Hill and stocked it with a dozen prostitutes. Business boomed and he soon had three to four houses going. And just below Signal Hill on Cottonwood Creek, he built a large, elaborate still. Shine got his brother to take over the girls so he could devote his considerable talents to bootlegging, opening a place just outside the city limits of Stinnett, north of Borger, called the Blue Moon. Within a year, he dominated the bootlegging and prostitution businesses in the Texas Panhandle. He had literally killed off his competition. At one time estimates were that he had two hundred prostitutes and fifty bootleggers working for him, and he claimed to have every lawman and judge in the area in his pocket. That could have been true since none of his places were ever raided until the Texas Rangers came along in 1927.

One of his bootleggers, Bill Parks, was caught stealing moonshine by Popejoy and selling in a place of his own near Electric City. Then Parks and three other men tried to kill Shine by running him off the road one night. Parks shot him at point-blank range in the forehead with a pistol, but the bullet cut a bloody path upward and about all Shine got out of it was an enormous headache. Parks, however, thinking he had killed Popejoy, suggested to his three companions that they take the body to some isolated place and burn it up with gasoline. When they stopped to get a can of gasoline, Popejoy escaped. Two weeks later, he walked into the Stinnett Post Office and killed Parks with two blasts from a shotgun.

He was jailed and the murder trial was transferred to Miami, Texas. While he was there, the Texas Rangers raided his underground still and blew it up with dynamite. Two weeks following the raid, two sheriff's deputies were gunned down in Borger and there was considerable speculation that their deaths were the result of Shine not being notified of the raid by the Rangers. The murder trial ended in an acquittal when his attorney produced Shine's Stetson showing a hole in the sweatband matching the scar on his forehead. Self defense.

Two years later Shine was accused of killing Johnny Holmes, the district attorney, but on the night of Holmes' murder, witnesses said Shine was in the Blue Moon, so nothing came of the accusation. A couple of weeks later the Blue Moon burned to the ground and a charred body was found inside. Everyone supposed it was Shine.

However, on March 15, 1932, a Stinnett banker, G.W. Newsom, was robbed at gunpoint and relieved of $5,000. The robber was Shine Popejoy, who had been hiding out in Obar, New Mexico. Three days later, Shine robbed the bank in Plemons, getting only $100.

He was captured and brought to trial on an old indictment for liquor violation and given two years in Huntsville. However, his lawyers appealed the sentence to a higher court. While free on bond on the appeal for the old indictment and the robbery of Newsom and the Plemons bank holdup, Shine walked into the Stinnett bank with three Oklahoma friends and robbed it. Shine took off for Oklahoma, stealing a car in Stinnett, tried to rob the Plemons bank on his way out of the Panhandle, held up a filling station in Pampa, killed and robbed a man in McLean, and ditched the stolen car in Elk City, Oklahoma.

He was captured again in Oklahoma City, and returned to the Stinnett jail. On January 15, 1933, Shine, armed with a .45 calibre revolver and a .32 calibre derringer, tried to escape. After an exchange of shots with the jailer, Shine died on a jail cell floor, using his last living breath, so it's said, shouting obscenities at the jailer.

His brother, Torrance, charged several times with liquor violations, finally moved to San Jon, New Mexico, where he is said to have shot five to six men in a bar he owned. The last report of him was that he was in a sanitarium in Tucumcari, New Mexico.

If Shine were the king of the bootleggers, then "Two Gun" Dick Herwig was the prince of the city's whiskey line.

Herwig, a convicted murderer from Oklahoma, was named chief deputy by his friend Mayor Miller. He, in turn, named other deputies to serve under men he had known in other oil boom towns in Oklahoma and Texas. The story about town was that Herwig made enough from his illicit activities to buy "a pardon" from an Oklahoma judge. Price: $40,000. No one ever proved the truth of the tale one way or the other, but Herwig isn't known to have gone back to Oklahoma from Borger.

He brought new meaning to the word "intimidation." He wore two pearl handled six-shooters and had a penchant for pistol whipping, particularly when his victim was too drunk to defend himself or when tied to the jail's trotline. Some citizens figured he was too cowardly to fight fair. He also kept one to two very mean German shepherds with him when making his rounds to collect

35

payoffs from prostitutes and saloon keepers.

Under Herwig's direction the city's beer and whiskey lines were set up. Prohibition to Herwig meant opportunity, and he took advantage of it. There were liquor joints in every block, some masquerading as cafes, gambling halls, rooming houses, or "drug stores." The so-called drug stores had a few cartons of cheap cigarettes in stock, some cheap brands of patent medicines, and other standard merchandise around to keep up appearances. A slot machine or two brought in the trade. Booze could be purchased in the back room for fifty cents a drink for whiskey or fifty cents a bottle for beer.

Bootleggers who bought line whiskey and beer were protected by Herwig and his enforcers. They paid fifteen dollars a gallon for whiskey and four dollars a case for the line's special brand of "choc" beer, identified by its peculiar chalky taste. The line's customers found it was better to buy line whiskey and beer than not to. Herwig doctored his product and had his own chemist run tests on it. If he found some "wild cat whiskey" being sold, the bootlegger ended up getting rapped across the head with Herwig's pistols or his place of business "mysteriously" burned down or was raided.

Herwig, fortunately for Borger's citizens, didn't last long as a law enforcement officer. The appearance of the Texas Rangers in 1927 put an end to his intimidating ways, and he left town. It wouldn't have surprised anyone if a band had played a farewell march and the citizenry declared a holiday. Herwig wouldn't be missed.

Herwig located downstate in another oil town, where his welcome wore out quite quickly, too. The Rangers there encouraged him to keep moving. He did, going across the Texas line into New Mexico, where he opened a roadhouse with a large lettered sign out front — EIGHT MILES FROM TEXAS RANGERS — which was about as smart as waving a red flag in front of a Spanish fighting bull.

36

DEPUTY PERRY CHUCULATE was killed when he tried to capture the Kimes boys.

CHIEF DEPUTY M.L. LARIMORE.

H.H. MURRAY, former chief of Police, Plainview, Texas, wrote several stories about Borger's early days.

DEPUTY A.L. TERRY may have been killed deliberately by bandits who knew he was coming.

37

Captain William Lee (Bud) Wright of Company D took umbrage at this affront to the Rangers and had himself and his entire company commissioned as one-dollar-a-year federal officers. They then crossed the state line and raided the place, putting Herwig out of business. What happened to this two gun "police officer"after that wasn't determined.

Armed robbery and hijacking were common in Borger, so much so that an aroused citizenry organized several vigilante-type committees armed with pistols, shotguns, and anything else they could fight with. Their battle cry was "Shoot to Kill!" and they posted warnings to travelers:

> *Don't come in from the fields after dark. Don't stop to fix a tire on the road. Don't stop to help parked cars. Don't fall for the old stunt of a pocket book, or a tire lying in the road. Don't go for your gun if the other fellow has the drop; but if you get an even break, open up and shoot to kill.*

The oil men were told that to "take the life of the dope-head, hijacker, and jake-gurgler before they took yours is the only way to end the menace." Others were told, "Mob him and let his relatives weep because he didn't get a trial."

Although the vigilante committees may have been organized in theory, they apparently didn't operate in fact. Even with their hard talk, they weren't much of a deterent to the criminals operating quite openly in Borger.

Generally, the feeling was similar to that of a man named Snider, who arrived in Borger in 1926, when it was a city of mud streets:

You didn't get off in the back streets, when you

came to town. You stayed in the light because somebody would take you and they wasn't particular how they took you.

The bad guys didn't always win, however. C.C. McClelland told of a hijacking on the Hardiger lease on the river below Phillips.

This fellow was coming up to the Phillips camp, and there were some fellows in a Ford car, and they couldn't make the hill. They got to talking to him. He said, 'Well, turn her around and back her up. You can make it that way. Turn the Ford around and back up the hill.'

One fellow said to him, 'Well,' he said, 'turn her around. You think we can make it?'

'Well,' he said, 'you've got every advantage in the world. Your gas tank's all right that way. The other way you don't get no gas.'

So they finally robbed the fellow and took his money away from him. But he was a pretty smart guy. He had a pistol on him, but they didn't discover it. So they jumped in the Ford and started to back her up the hill, you know, and they got up. They was going up all right, but they got too close to the edge and went over the edge a way and they couldn't get any further, you know. So he was walkin' right up the hill behind 'em. He got up and saw they was stuck. He pulled out the pistol and stuck it in the old boy's ribs and said, 'Give me my money back. I'll kill you both right here and shoot a hole in the gas tank and set it afire.'

They give him back his watch and money, and then he marched them right up to the Phillips camp and turned them over to the law.

Richard R. Moore in his book, *West Texas After The Discovery of Oil*, wrote that "oil scouts were constantly harassed by road agents who would stop them by erecting a roadblock and then take the scouts' automobiles and money. In the summer of 1926, this hijacking became such a popular occupation that it seriously interfered with the drilling operations in the Borger field. More than a dozen drilling rigs were closed down one June night when four bandits rounded up twenty-seven drillers and tool dressers and relieved them of sixteen watches and $400 in cash. The four robbers, armed with two revolvers each, visited the rigs one at a time and at gunpoint forced the oil men to accompany them to a ravine. Here the victims were assembled under the charge of one guard while the other three bandits continued their roundup. The lone guard was a short, partly masked man who 'twirled a six-shooter with lightning rapidity around a practiced thumb, then snapped it back into aim,' informing the prisoners, 'if any of you want to commit suicide, just raise up.' When the robbery was completed, the oil men suffered the final ignominy of having rocks tossed at them when they ran from the ravine."

Hijacking was relatively easy because there were few roads into Borger during those early days. Most anyone who wanted to go to Borger just headed out across the prairie, more or less taking a chance of arriving at his or her destination with personal belongings still intact. Few of the hijackers were caught since they could easily fade into the surrounding country where tracking was nigh unto impossible. And anyway, the law enforcement agencies had more on their plate than they could swallow, what with the dope peddling, illegal booze, easy women, and nearly nightly stickups going on.

One armed robbery in Borger, however, incensed a Plainview lawman enough that he would not rest until the crooks were found and jailed.

On January 15, 1927, sometime between 9 p.m. and 10 p.m., A.A. Monte, owner of a small filling station a block east of the Whittenburg Post Office, was making out invoices for auto accessories. His small son was playing nearby, Monte's wife, Edna, was visiting with Mrs. M.A. Chaffee in the station's living quarters at back. Through the doorway, they could hear father and son talking.

Suddenly the door of the station slammed open, and a harsh voice said, "Get in there and keep your hands up. And you (indicating Monte), stick'm up! If anyone moves, I'll blow the daylights out of you."

The two women, unseen by the robber, got to their feet, Mrs. Monte went to a bedside table and picked up a new .38 Smith and Wesson her husband had given her. She stepped to the door of the office. On the opposite side of the room, with arms in the air, stood Monte, M.A. Chaffee, and the young boy. They were staring at a masked man who was holding a gun on them. At the cash register was another masked man. Both had their backs to Mrs. Monte.

She aimed the revolver at the one at the register and pulled the trigger. She missed, and he whirled around and shot twice. Mrs. Monte died almost instantly. The robber then picked up Mrs. Monte's gun and stuck it into his pocket. Seeing Mrs. Chaffee he motioned her into the station to stand by the others. He then continued rifling the register, then went into the bedroom and ransacked it, thinking, perhaps, there was more money to be found

He found nothing, and with the fifty dollars he got from the register, he and his companion left, disappearing into the darkness.

Chaffee, recovering first from the shock of the killing, called Captain Tom Hickman of the Texas Rangers, but he was out investigating the burglary of a Santa Fe Railway warehouse from which $2,500 in cigarettes had been taken. Chaffee finally got hold of the Ranger captain, and he and two other Rangers, Purvis and Kirby, and a police officer named Reddell, drove to the service station.

Chaffee told the officers that prior to the shooting he had been at home listening to the radio when the two bandits burst in on him demanding his money. They got $100 from his wallet, then marched him across the street to the Monte filling station.

The Rangers began gathering what clues they could to the indentity of the robbers. They learned that a car had driven away hurriedly shortly after the robbers had left the station. That meant a third man. They found a footprint in a patch of oil-soaked dust. It had been made by a man wearing a size seven shoe, and that was enough to bring in bloodhounds.

H.H. Murray, chief of police of Plainview, Texas, had three bloodhounds, and since he was the nearest officer with dogs, he was called.

When he finally arrived the next day, the Rangers had some description to go by — the bandit covering Monte and Chaffee had black eyes, was tall and muscular; the killer was fair, slender, with blue eyes and light brown hair. The latter also had the .38 Smith & Wesson owned by Mrs. Monte.

Murray's dogs picked up the scent and took off through the breaks. They followed a ditch, then took off down a draw, stopping by a derrick. A man came running toward them and wanted to know what was going on. When told, he said his car had been stolen, a blue Plymouth. The Rangers put out a pick-up order on the car.

Captain Hickman suggested they try to trace the revolver. No criminal, he reasoned, was going to keep such incriminating evidence long. "He'll get rid of it, and I know just where he'll go — a pawnshop at Pantex."

Murray and Hickman drove to Pantex, a cluster of wild shacks two miles from Borger, and stopped at a rambling building. Hickman told the woman, the owner,

TEXAS RANGERS AT Borger, Texas, April 17, 1927, standing in front of the jail, which contained the dreaded "trotline." 1. Not Identified. 2. Private Hickman. 3. W. W. Taylor. 4. A.P. Cummings, 5. Capt. Tom Hickman. 6. Capt. Bill Sterling. 7. Capt. Frank Hamer. 8. Mayor Miller of Borger. 9. Charles Davis. Standing: Pvt. Purvis and Pvt. Ballard.

(Photo from Trails and Trials of a Texas Ranger, William W. Sterling. University of Oklahoma Press, 1968.)

what he wanted, and she produced a .38 Smith and Wesson.

"A couple of guys came in with it early this morning," she said. "Just supposed they were on the up-and-up, so I took the gun."

Hickman paid her for the revolver and on the way out to the car, he snorted, "On the up-and-up. That's a laugh!"

They finally traced the men to a rundown rooming house in Borger, but got there too late. Hickman felt the men were "holed up in the breaks," and he asked for a posse of local officers to hunt for them. They finally found an oil driller who remembered seeing a car parked by an abandoned shack, and the Rangers headed toward the area. The car was gone, but they did find footprints of men wearing size ten shoes. Two men with the same size shoes, a fact that puzzled them. A set of small footprints convinced them they had the three men pegged.

More than fifty suspects were rounded up, but none proved to be the robbers. Then Sheriff Bill Thompson of Amarillo called Captain Hickman and said he had two suspects in the Monte case in jail. Since Hickman was tied down in Borger, he asked Chief Murray to stop by the Amarillo jail and question the men.

Murray arrived in Amarillo to learn that the arrest of the two men came about when Mr. and Mrs. J.W. Gladstone, who lived in a 16th Street apartment, heard the two men talking in a room adjacent to theirs. The written statement showed the conversation as they remembered it:

"I wish I hadn't been forced to hit that woman."

"Wonder if she died?"

"Maybe it's just as well if she did; but I'm tellin' you I don't like to kill a woman."

"The men were cleaning guns, to judge by the sounds in their room," the Gladstone's statement said. "Finally they went out, but were back in a couple of hours."

"They nearly nabbed us that time!"

"Yeah, it was a close call!"

The Gladstones called the sheriff and the two men were taken into custody. One had a .45 Colt, the other a .32 Smith and Wesson. Their descriptions were close, but neither wore size seven or size ten shoes. They were not the men.

To Murray the case appeared hopeless, and he knew he would get no help from the Borger police, who "would make no effort to solve the mystery." Borger was out of his territory anyway, and he returned to his duties in Plainview.

Murray never gave up, though. He knew that gangsters, with headquarters in Borger and nearby Signal Hill, were operating throughout the Panhandle. "Plainview was not an oil town, but it was between the Wink and San Angelo fields and was receiving the impact of an astonishing amount of crime. It was evident we were bucking a big ring of well organized, well protected thugs who knew the ropes."

Several weeks went by, and, as Murray knew it would, nothing was done by the Borger sheriff's department or police about the Monte shooting. "Even the two bullets taken from the murdered woman's body had been lost and forgotten — the only real evidence we had against the killer."

Then, through an informant, Murray came up with a name: Scotty Hyden, a bank robber. Hyden was slight of build, blue eyed, a smooth talker, and always handsomely dressed. He was the Beau Brummel of the gangster set.

Murray arrived in Borger on March 20, 1927, and learned that Hyden was staying at the Marland Hotel under an alias, Harold Ray. Murray arrested Hyden and took him to the city jail. "It was a foregone conclusion that the minute my back was turned he would buy himself out, but I figured the 'escape' would not take place before dark. So, to forestall any undue haste on the part of the police, I announced that I would be in Borger two days. As a matter of fact, I expected to leave within the hour."

Murray had not gone two blocks when he heard shots. He turned to see his prisoner running from the jail with two men hot on his heels, "both of them shooting at the ground." Hyden ran into a drugstore near the police station, and Murray, knowing he would head for the back door, went around the alley. All back doors were locked in Borger, and Murray was not surprised to see Hyden plunge through a window, shattering glass in every direction. "He was half blinded by blood from cuts on his face and he ran straight toward me. Just then, a constable stepped from a shack at the end, and failing to recognize Hyden, helped me capture the outlaw. As we turned into the street, a policeman came up and started kicking Hyden.

"What are you kicking him now for?" I asked. "You should have done that before you turned him loose."

Murray learned later that as soon as he had left the jail, Hyden had been taken to a bank next door and had withdrawn $250 — the price of his release.

The Plainview chief of police took Hyden to Panhandle to a "safe jail." He learned then that Hyden might have been in on the robbery of the Santa Fe warehouse a couple of months prior.

Meanwhile, Clayton Tontz and his brother, Frazier, were arrested in Amarillo. Clayton was wanted for the murder of John Langley, a prominent Amarillo druggist. When Murray, who had been told of the arrests, saw Clayton, he felt that maybe he had Hyden's partner in the Monte killing. "He was tall, broad shouldered, with black curly hair, and eyes as completely black as I've ever seen. He was a dead ringer for the description the Pantex woman had given Hickman and me of one of the men who pawned Mrs. Monte's gun."

Tontz was not talking, but the Amarillo sheriff told Murray about Frazier, held in another office. Murray went in to see him and came face to face with Clayton's twin. The Tontz' both wore size ten shoes. Murray knew he had his men.

Hyden confessed to the warehouse robbery, implicating the Tontz brothers, but he would not confess to Mrs. Monte's killing. A special agent for the Santa Fe, W.B. Jones, put Hyden on a train for Stinnett, and just as the train was gathering speed out of Amarillo, Hyden broke through a window and jumped. No trace was found of him. He had managed a clean getaway.

Clayton and Frazier Tontz were ordered arrested for bank robbery, and were in the Stinnett jail. The two brothers and another criminal, "Whitey" Walker, overpowered a jailer and escaped into Oklahoma. Walker eventually killed Clayton following a bank robbery. Frazier was killed while trying to escape from Sheriff John Russell of Okmulgee, Oklahoma.

Murray heard about Hyden again when the Carbon, Texas, bank was robbed of 1,000 unsigned bank notes. Hyden's accomplice, E.V. Allen, was finally arrested, and Hyden then picked up. Hyden and Allen were convicted and Hyden got life imprisonment and Allen, death. They were sent to Huntsville.

Hyden escaped again, and headed for the Hawaiian Islands. He remained there a year, but wrote his girl friend, living in Wichita Falls, that he was returning to the States. Murray found out about the letter after tracing the girl down, and learned the route Hyden would take. He came into California, then El Paso, and on to Dallas, and it was there Murray captured him once again. Hyden was returned to Huntsville, and after a few years came down with tuberculosis. He was sent to his home near Clovis, New Mexico, to die.

A large car theft ring operated in Borger, and it was successful because many of the city's so-called "law enforcement" people and bureaucrats were deeply involved with it.

Cars stolen in other oil towns, such as McCamey or

Ranger, or in Oklahoma, most likely ended up in Borger, where there would be an almost instant sale or where auto parts were exchanged or where the car was stripped completely and the parts sold elsewhere.

Here's the way it would work. The "law" collected reward money for recovering stolen autos. Suppose a car was stolen in Amarillo and the Borger police were notified. The next day the Amarillo police would be called and told the car had been found, but that it had been necessary to put on a new set of tires or other repairs had to be made before the car could be moved. When the Amarillo lawmen came to Borger to get the car, they'd be handed a bill for the repairs plus the request for the reward of $25 to $50. In all likelihood the new tires had come from another stolen car of the same make, thus this particular racket was an efficient method of getting rid of stolen goods.

Usually the cars were brought into one of the "gyp garages" in the area and repainted, parts interchanged, and new papers made out. The latter took some help from city hall. However, this was also the weakest link in the chain, because it was through the new titles that many of the cars were recovered.

Narcotics, booze, girls, and graft in many forms were part of the town that Ace built. This isn't to say that everyone who lived in Borger was all bad. It was a boom-town situation, and there probably were more "good" people living there wanting to make an honest living than "bad" people making a dishonest living. Ace just wasn't all that discriminating when it came to making as much money as he could in the town he started.

When all the sites had been sold in Borger, Ace looked for other towns to build in the Texas Panhandle. After all, real estate was still his prime business.

He talked with A. S. Stinnett of Amarillo, and when the talking was finished, Ace bought 960 acres at the Stinnett townsite, twelve miles north of the town of Borger. He subdivided, set up his tent, and repeated his earlier success. Within thirty days, he took in $250,000 on his $100,000 investment, and by the time the last plot had been sold, he had grossed another $1,250,000. After checking his books, Ace told his friends that "real estate is a better business than oil."

A.P., as many called him, regarded Stinnett as his swan song as a town builder. Although just in his late thirties, he wanted to retire and devote time to his investments and other business enterprises.

Ace couldn't stay out of real estate altogether, however. He bought forty-four sections of land in the Gruver community, and gave that area a boost when he cut fourteen sections into small farms to sell. He kept the remainder to raise wheat, planting some 19,000 acres and realizing as many as thirty-five to forty bushels per acre.

Borger said it cost him a dollar a bushel to grow wheat on his Missouri farm, but only thirty cents a bushel in the Texas Panhandle. "Down in Missouri, I can plow seven acres a day. Out here I can plow fifty acres for the same cost that I plow seven there."

Ace also owned a string of wheat elevators on the Texas North Plains, and planned to build a $300,000 elevator in Amarillo. He had interests in New Mexico and Texas oil fields.

During September, 1927, Ace, Judge W.R. Goodwin, W.C. Womble, and J.T. Hodges as stockholders opened the First State Bank in Stinnett. Borger was president; John R. Miller, vice president; J.T. Peyton, cashier; and R.A. Franks, assistant cashier.

Bank robbery was not uncommon in those early days, and the Stinnett bank had its share of robberies. One school student said that the way he learned to read was when the teacher wrote on the blackboard every Friday: "The bank has been robbed." Well, not quite that often, but often enough to be irritating.

Perhaps the most sensational story about the First State Bank was the alleged embezzlement of $6,601.80

by R. A. Franks on November 15, 1929. Arrested with him were Torrance A. Popejoy, J.W. Adams of Clarendon, and Bert Smith, a cotton gin owner at Lelia Lake.

The money belonged to J.T. Peyton, the bank's cashier.

Either Franks was gullible or Popejoy had some hold over him, but either way, Popejoy talked Franks into taking the money for some purpose involving Adams and Smith.

Smith denied knowledge of the crime.

Although everyone was arrested, no one went to jail for it. The money was recovered in Lelia Lake, and on October 25, 1935, the case against Franks and the others was dismissed for "insufficient evidence."

Then, on June 16, 1930, Ace started the Borger State Bank, naming himself as president; a son, Phil, vice president; and Peyton, cashier. Unfortunately, the bank failed, causing a minor panic among the town's businessmen and small depositors and a lot of hard feelings generally.

Ace was indicted for receiving funds into the defunct bank after it was determined to be insolvent. Twice his trial ended in hung juries. During the third trial, however, he was convicted and given a two year prison sentence. He appealed.

One man was particularly bitter over the bank's failure. He was Arthur Huey, Hutchinson County tax collector. To begin with, Huey wasn't fond of Ace and the bank failure only intensified his dislike. He finally ended up shooting Ace.

There are two versions why.

Ace's descendants say that he was generous to a fault, particularly with friends and acquaintances. He was known to have paid the bails of many when they found themselves jailed for infractions of the law. It was common knowledge that he did it. Huey, not exactly recognized as a model among tax collectors, was jailed for embezzlement, and being without ready funds, asked Ace to bail him out of jail.

Ace, figuring that Huey needed to be taught a lesson, refused, telling Huey he'd just let him stay in jail overnight and hope that he would learn something from the experience. Huey was angered by the refusal and treatment, and when he was released, he went hunting for Ace. He found him in the post office and shot him dead.

According to witnesses, Ace was in the post office standing by his box getting his mail when Huey came in with pistol in hand. Ace dropped his mail and started backing off as Huey shouted, "You son of a bitch, get your gun!" Then, he fired two shots and Ace fell to the floor. Huey fired four more times, grabbed Borger's gun and fired three more shots. Then Huey partially picked Borger up from the floor and said, "Well, you S.O.B., I got you this time!"

One of the nine shots fired hit Lloyd Duncan, farm boss for the Magnolia Petroleum Company, in the leg. At the time, the wound wasn't considered serious. However, complications set in, and Duncan died on September 5, 1934, while funeral services were being held for Ace.

Ace was forty-eight years old when Huey, with malice aforethought, pumped seven bullets into him, two into the chest and five into the back. All but two passed completely through his body, and Dr. Larry Hensen said that "any one of six of the seven wounds would have been fatal." Five of the bullets were fired from Huey's Colt .45 and four from Ace's .44. Neither man had a permit to carry a gun. The shooting took place on August 31, 1934.

Trial for Huey was held during the December term, 1934, in the District Court of Hemphill County. A change of venue had been asked for and granted. Because of Ace's popularity, it was unlikely Huey would have received a fair and impartial trial in Hutchinson County.

Huey claimed he had been "jibed out of the money he had in the Borger State Bank." Huey also had been among those who relentlessly demanded prosecution of Borger for the bank's failure. A second story circulated was that Ace reportedly said to a man named Chenault, "I have got your friend, Huey, where I want him now. I mean just what I say, I have got him where I want him. I am going to kill him before night or he will kill me."

Just what he was referring to isn't known, but it could have had something to do with Huey's double bookkeeping. However, that's a matter of speculation and no definite proof is available to verify the conjecture.

When Ace's threat was repeated to Huey, the tax collector armed himself and went hunting for the city's founding father, supposedly to reach some agreement and avoid personal trouble. That's what Huey said in court, anyway. Huey apparently convinced the jury that it was a matter of self defense, because, on December 15, he was found not guilty.

That isn't the end of Huey's story, however.

Three years later Huey told the Hutchinson County sheriff he had been robbed by highwaymen as he was driving from Panhandle to Borger with county funds. He said he had been tied up, but managed to get loose. By then the bandits had disappeared.

The sheriff called in the Texas Rangers to help work on the case, and the Rangers proved that Huey had tied himself up, taken the money, and told a false story. Huey was sentenced to four years for embezzlement. He entered the penitentiary at Huntsville on February 26, 1937, as Number 84572. He was paroled on July 17, 1939.

3

The Set Up:
The Death of Two Cops

It was 11:20 a.m., March 30, 1927.

There was a touch of spring in the air and Pampa businessman, J.E. Murfee was at peace with himself. Sales the day before had amounted to a healthy $1,100, and he was ready to take the money to the bank.

He finished filling out the bank slip, shoved the money and checks into the small canvas bag, told his clerk to mind the store and headed for the First National down the street.

The time was 11:35 a.m.

When Murfee opened the bank's door, two things impressed him, although neither fully registered immediately. One was the unusual quiet. No machines clacking. No talking. No paper rustling. The second was the nattily dressed young man by the door.

He learned the significance of both shortly.

The man closed the door behind him and said politely, but firmly, "I'll relieve you of that." The gun in his hand brought a quick response from Murfee. He handed the bag over.

Then the man asked a peculiar question, considering the circumstances, "Is it insured?"

Murfee shook his head no.

To the surprise of everyone, the polite young man handed the bag back, saying somewhat apologetically, "I can't take it then." With that Murfee was motioned toward the vault where twenty-five employees and customers were huddled.

Two other conservatively dressed men finished shoving money from the tellers' locations into a cement bag one had picked up off the street outside the bank.

"I can't get it all in here," one complained.

There was nothing in the bank they could use so one of them walked casually across the street and bought a small suitcase. They money did fit into that. All $32,650 of it.

The four unmasked robbers had entered the bank at 11:30 a.m. One remained by the front door, a second walked to the back door, and two approached D. L. Vickers, cashier. A fifth man, the driver, stayed outside in a new Buick limousine.

"What can I do for you, sir?" Vickers asked.

The answer was obvious when he saw the gun in the "customer's" hand.

The bandits worked swiftly. Calmly.

When they finished ransacking the vault and cash drawers, they herded the customers and employees into the vault. One of the robbers handed Vickers a screwdriver and showed him how to escape from the vault.

"It won't take you long," he said, and with that the bandits closed the heavy steel door. Then they walked outside to their car and drove off in the direction of Clarendon.

The whole robbery of the Pampa bank took thirteen minutes.

Within ten minutes Vickers had gotten the vault door open and notified police. The chase was on!

Gray County Sheriff Graves notified officers throughout the area to set up roadblocks, and from the descriptions of the witnesses he put out the word that the bandits were "Whitey" Walker, Ed Bailey, Owen Edwards, Matt Kimes, and Ray Terrell. He was only partially right. It seemed that anytime anything went wrong in the area Kimes and Terrell were blamed for it. Actually the robbers were Walker, Bailey, Ace Pendleton, Fred Nave, and Edwards.

Any one of those names was enough to make anyone cautious in approaching them. They weren't as genteel as the bank customers and employees thought.

A carload of deputies took off after the robbers, believing they were headed toward Clarendon. The fugitives had doubled back after a few blocks, however, and headed toward Borger. The law all headed in the wrong direction, and no matter which side road, back road, or highway they took, it seemed as if the earth had opened and swallowed the bandits' car.

Although the bandits were headed toward Borger, it was learned later that that town wasn't their destination. Instead, they turned off the Borger road six miles from Pampa and went to a farm house a mile or so down the road.

The farm was owned by W. E. Archer and his sister.

It was noon, and the Archers were eating lunch when they heard a car come up the driveway, pass the house, and drive right into the garage. Perplexed, the Archers started to walk outside when the five bandits pushed their way into the kitchen.

"Sit down, both of you, and don't start nothing," one told the two. "If you do, we'll blow your heads off!"

The robbers locked the front and back doors, pulled down window shades and arranged the lace curtains so no one could see in from the outside.

Everyone sat. No one talked.

From time to time the intruders glanced at their watches, but no one said anything. Then, about 2 p.m., a car drove up to the front gate and stopped. Presently, the heavy tread of a man sounded on the porch. One of the robbers lifted his gun in warning, looking with cold brown eyes at the Archers. There was a rap; then another, longer and louder.

"No one's home, I guess," called a voice from the porch.

"Doesn't look like it," came another from the car. "I told you this was a waste of time."

"Yeah, guess it was." With that, the man at the door walked back to the car. It drove off in a cloud of dust.

Everyone in the room relaxed. The leader, a lean dark-complexioned man, smiled coldly. "We'll wait," he said.

The afternoon wore on. Darkness came, and the bandits got to their feet and without a word ushered the frightened Archers into a closet and locked the door. Then the bandits left the house, got into their car, and drove away.

Archer broke out of the closet and raced to the phone, only to find the bandits had cut the wires. He was unable to notify the sheriff until morning, and by then it was too late.

March 30 apparently had been a good day for robbing banks. One at Palacio, Texas, and another at Shattuck, Oklahoma, were hit successfully. That alone made law enforcement agencies rather jumpy.

Potter County Sheriff Wiley Pollard traced four men through Claude, Goodnight, and Clarendon, thinking they were the Pampa bank robbers. They weren't. Three men driving a coupe were arrested in Wheeler, forty-six miles southeast of Pampa. They weren't the bank robbers either.

Amarillo Chief of Police H.L. Gaither thought the description of the Pampa bandits tallied closely with that of four escaped convicts from the Oklahoma penitentiary. They were thought to be in the Amarillo area. They weren't.

All in all it was a frustrating chase in which the bad guys won.

Or so they thought.

Sheriff Graves and two deputies arrived at the Archer farm early the next morning and traced the car tracks to the Borger-Pampa Highway, which was unpaved. Two miles west, the car turned off toward the Canadian River breaks. There was no road going that way, but with careful driving, the rough terrain could be crossed.

"There's no longer any mystery where they're heading," the sheriff observed. "The oil field."

Graves went to Borger for reinforcements, and the large posse began checking every arroyo, shack, ditch, and house throughout the rough breaks. The search lasted for eighteen hours and they came up with nothing.

On April 1, a new development entered the case.

Henry Fields, a well driller, reported to the Borger sheriff that he'd seen two dead men lying beside the Whittenburg Road, a mile out of town. There was an abandoned car nearby.

Sheriff Joe Ownbey, District Attorney Curtis Douglas, and two Texas Rangers, Ballard and McCormack, drove out to the spot. They found two police officers, D.P. Kenyon and A.L. Terry, dead. Kenyon had been shot in the head. Terry was shot through the right eye. Both had died instantly.

Two loaded guns lay on the ground between them.

Checking the guns, Sheriff Ownbey said, "There's been some switching of guns here. I gave Terry my white-handled pistol yesterday, but it ain't here now."

He was to find it later.

Douglas found some currency wrappings nearby.

From the outward appearance, it looked as if the two policeman had been in on a division of the take from the Pampa bank robbery. However, Douglas didn't believe so. "If that were the case, they wouldn't have left the wrappers. No, it's a plant."

They finally concluded that Kenyon and Terry had been tipped off that the bandits were going to divide the stolen money in that location and drove out to capture them. They failed.

Mrs. Percy May, who lived a short distance from the murder scene, helped establish the time of the shooting. She said she'd been awakened about 3:15 a.m. by shots and loud voices and a car driving away.

When the coroner arrived, the sheriff and Rangers returned to Borger to question Hugh Walker, "Whitey's" brother. They reasoned that while he may not have had anything to do with the robbery, he'd probably know something about it.

After some tough questioning, Walker said he didn't know who robbed the Pampa bank, but why not ask Ed Bailey and Whitey themselves. They were in the bedroom in back of his drugstore.

Awakened, Whitey and Bailey denied any knowledge of the robbery and killings, so Sheriff Ownbey took a different tack. "Do either of you have my white-handled pistol?" They denied seeing that, too.

Whitey, meanwhile, had sat down on the edge of the bed and started putting on his socks. The sheriff, on a whim, told him to get up. He lifted the mattress and there it was, a surprise to no one.

All three men were arrested, placed under $50,000 bond each, and taken to the Stinnett jail.

A nasty rumor, probably with some basis in fact, started around town that Kenyon and Terry might have been set up for the killing. The two had been doing some sleuthing on their own, and, according to the talk, apparently had found strong evidence that some of their fellow officers were "on the take." It may have been that they were about to bring the corruption within the police and sheriff's departments out into the open, and those supplementing their pay weren't about to have a good thing stopped.

Gen. Jacob Wolters of the Texas National Guard said a couple of years after the killings that he was convinced the police officers were "assassinated." He came

58

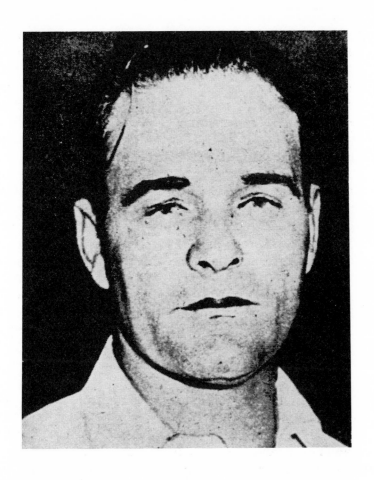

MATT KIMES gloried in making headlines. He was right up there
with Bonnie and Clyde in notoriety.

to that conclusion following testimony brought out during a court of inquiry into the corruption in Borger generally.

Their deaths, with all indications that neither had a chance to defend himself, didn't set well with the more law-abiding citizens in town. Once the word got out that the Walkers and Bailey were in jail, forty to fifty carloads of angry men headed toward Stinnett.

Tipped off that the mob was on its way, the sheriff and two deputies rushed to the jail and took the three crooks out and drove them to a remote spot in a canyon north of town, where they remained under guard.

The sheriff returned to Stinnett to find his other deputies and Texas Rangers facing nearly two hundred angry men.

"We're taking over!" the mob yelled. "We want those killers!"

The sheriff drove his car to within a few feet of the jail, blinked his lights to get the attention of the men.

"Now, men, you'd as well go on home. Your men are gone. They're miles away by now," he said.

"We don't believe it. Get out of the way, sheriff, we're going to get them!"

Just then more officers and Rangers arrived and formed a triple guard around the jail. With the formidable array of weapons facing them, the angry men slowly dispersed. However, they didn't give up. They knew that Matt Kimes and Ray Terrell were still on the loose, and they started hunting for them, not knowing that neither of these two were involved in the robbery.

Kimes and Terrell knew that, but they also knew that the posse didn't know that, so they got out of town. These two were familiar figures around Signal Hill, mostly a hangout for the hard-case criminals in the area. Kimes, also, was seen around city hall regularly talking with some of the local law. He seemed to have an immunity from arrest, which tells you something of the character of the early law in Borger.

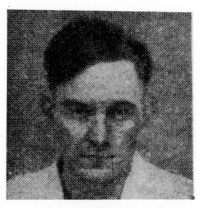

WHITEY WALKER was one of the premier bank robbers operating in several states. He was killed during an escape attempt from the penitentiary at Huntsville, Texas.

SCOTTY HYDEN, who specialized in robbing banks, was also an escape artist. He died of TB in his home near Clovis, N.M.

E.V. ALLEN, a bank robber, was given a death sentence for helping a wanted man.

MRS. WHITEY WALKER was no angel.

The posse was divided into groups and a sweep was made through the oilfield and breaks. The sheriff and his men stayed together. They found the Buick used in the bank robbery near Electric City. On the floor was a pile of currency wrappers, enough to indicate that the money had been divided there.

They searched every house in the small community. Nothing. About daybreak a strong wind was blowing from the east and as they rounded a small hill, they inhaled the unmistakable odor of an operating still. They just followed their noses to a small cave screened by a grove of trees.

The posse moved in on the still, and when close enough, the sheriff yelled, "Come out with your hands up!" Guns were drawn, and the posse waited. "Come on out. We're not going to play games much longer!"

Suddenly, a muffled voice shouted, "Don't shoot. I'm comin'!" A very frightened man came out of the cave with his hands high.

With pistol pointing in the man's direction, Sheriff Ownbey said, "Just tell Kimes and Terrell to come out of there."

"They ain't here, sheriff. They was, but the lit out two hours ago."

"Where to?"

"They didn't say."

Disappointed, the sheriff said, "Well, we've got you anyway. Turning to a couple of his men, he directed them to bust up the still.

The manhunt moved to Borger. No trace of the bandits was found for several hours. Then a coupe parked on the Main Street was spotted. It was the car three bandits had driven away from nearby Signal Hill. Three? Kimes, Terrell, and who? It turned out to be Ace Pendleton. More currency wrappers were found on the floor.

The next lead came on April 5, when it was learned that Kimes and Terrell had stayed at the Marland Hotel the night before. The Pampa sheriff told the Rangers he thought Kimes and Terrell were holed up in a cabin between Pampa and Borger. This turned into a false lead.

Just when the Rangers seemed to be closing in on the two, they would get away. Ranger Frank Hamer finally figured out why — local police officers were tipping the fugitives off, thus giving them a good start before the Rangers showed.

Hamer, furious over the lack of cooperation, called Governor Moody, and the governor wired the Borger mayor to straighten things out in his town. *"If the officers of your town will not cooperate with the Rangers, maybe they'll cooperate with the National Guard."* The threat of martial law resulted in some reluctant cooperation.

On April 8, Kimes and Terrell were seen in Amarillo at the Tenth Street Cafe, and the next day, they were in Plainview. Police raced after them, but they always managed to get away in plenty of time. Finally, the chase slowed down, and it was learned a couple of weeks later that Kimes and Terrell were in Oklahoma.

Meanwhile, back in Stinnett, the Walkers had made bond, and promptly skipped town. Bailey, unable to make bond, agreed to testify against them — if they were caught again.

4

The Ghost Bandits

It began when two small boys rifled the candy counter in a little country store in Arkansas. One was an ingratiating youngster; sturdy open-eyed, with a wide artless grin. Had anything been done about it then . . . but a frail, overworked mother merely wept over them, a weary ineffectual father figured they didn't mean any harm and the good-natured storekeeper, accepting the case of eggs offered in payment, settled the matter with a package of gum for each culprit. So Matthew Kimes, age seven, sharing the spoils with less daring playmates, learned what it's like to be popular here.

— Human Detective Cases
January, 1947

It's understandable why Sheriff Graves thought Matt Kimes was one of the Pampa bank robbers. They were all so polite, and that was characteristic of Kimes, who might have qualified for the "Gentleman Bandit Award" if he hadn't been dangerous too. And the sheriff thought one of the descriptions fit Ray Terrell; but then,

THE FIRST NATIONAL Bank, Pampa, Texas, was robbed by
"gentlemen bandits," March 30, 1927. The robbers headed back
toward Borger.

STREET SCENE IN Rudy, Ark., where Matt Kimes, at the age of
seven, rifled a candy counter, starting his life of crime.

Photo from Human Detective Cases, January, 1947.

daylight robberies weren't his style, so he eventually was ruled out.

It is quite probable that the Pampa bank robbery was planned in lawless Signal Hill, generally regarded as a haven for bootleggers, fallen women, gamblers, and other undesirables who drifted into the oilfields.

Signal Hill, located a short way from Borger, had a brief, but uninhibited life, with its gambling dens, beer emporiums, brothels, dance halls, speakeasies, and other places of ill fame and function. At its peak, 1926-1927, it also had four drug stores, a bakery, an ice house, a dozen filling stations, a welding shop, a boiler shop, a hardware store, three oil supply houses, a meat market, movie house, bank (erected by Earl Thompson), several hotels, rooming houses, and sporting houses. One citizen recalled that the post office was the only place he would vouch for that didn't sell beer.

Signal Hill, too, was the hangout of several hardened, professional criminals, notably William (Whitey) Walker, Ray Terrell, Blackie Thompson, Ace Pendleton, Jack Whitehead, Owen Edwards, Torrence A. Popejoy, J.W. (Shine) Popejoy, and Matthew Kimes. In way of comparison, this lineup would rank favorably with Bonnie and Clyde, Al Capone, Baby Face Nelson, and John Dillinger.

While Walker, Terrell, Thompson, and the Popejoys had their moments of criminal glory, Kimes was the worst of the lot.

Matthew Edward Kimes was born in 1907 in Beggs, Oklahoma. His environment was hardly conducive to a "proper" upbringing. His father, Cornelius, finding honest labor not to his liking, ran a still. His mother raised corn and ran the small farm. His older brother, George, born in 1902, shoveled mash and peddled white lightning for his dad. Nellie, his sister, was no lady and got no better as the years went by. About the only other thing that could be said about her is that she was loyal to a fault where her brothers were concerned. She stood by

MATTHEW KIMES, left, and Ray Doolin after their capture in Arizona.

them no matter what they did. All in all, the Kimes family would never have been voted "Family of the Year" in Beggs.

George and Matt teamed up early in their life of crime. They stole a car in McAlester, Oklahoma, and were involved in various petty thefts. Then, with four others, they robbed a store at Non, Oklahoma, a small (now non-existent) community on the Coal-Hughes county line. They got away with three dollars cash and $14.50 in merchandise.

For that crime, George, Matt, and two others were sent to the Oklahoma penitentiary for two years. They served fourteen months, and it was there they met Roy Brandon, an early Twentieth Century Fagan, who always had a group of boys working for him. Brandon had a badly crippled body, but there wasn't anything wrong with his brain. He taught his boys what there was to know about thievery of every kind, and Matt was one of his better graduates.

Four months and thirteen days following their release, Matt and George were back in prison, charged with bank robbery and murder. The first bank they robbed was at Depew, Oklahoma, and they got away with an unspecified amount. The way the boys saw it was that Jesse James couldn't have done the job any better, and this gave them the confidence to try another bank. This one ended up with a shoot-out with the law and a murder charge against both of them.

Apparently the murder charge was dropped, because not many months later, Matt, George, and another young man entered the American State Bank in Covington, Oklahoma, cut the phone wires, herded the employees into the vault and walked out with $7,000. They crossed the street and repeated their success at the Covington National. Matt, the obvious leader, is supposed to have said, "Just give us the bank's money. We don't rob widows and orphans." Just how he was going to separate one from the other wasn't determined.

Anyway, they walked casually outside to a waiting sedan. The driver was Roy Brandon, their mentor at McAlester's penitentiary.

The town wasn't aware it had been robbed until a bank patron discovered the imprisoned employees in the first bank and gave the alarm. Everyone agreed that it was Matt and George, and when police put everything together, they went hunting for Brandon, too.

The bandits headed toward Sallisaw, Oklahoma, and Police Chief J.C. Woll called on Undersheriff Bert Cotton and Deputy Sheriff Perry Chuculate for help. They waited for the bank robbers at a turn in the road five miles out of town.

When the small Chevrolet sedan rounded the turn, the officers made a mistake, one that proved fatal for Chuculate and humiliating for Woll, who figured they were dealing with kids and wouldn't have any problem.

The car skidded to a halt, and Matt and George piled out, shooting. Chuculate, wounded by the first blast, bled to death. Cotton dived under an embankment and returned the fire. Woll, caught in the middle, didn't react fast enough, and the Kimes brothers yanked him off his feet, dumped him into the Chevrolet and sped off down the dusty road. It was 1 p.m.

At four that afternoon, Woll was released on a lonely stretch of road near the Arkansas line. Matt handed him a $20 bill, and reportedly said, with a touch of cynical humor, "That's to get you home. We don't aim to work a hardship on anybody." That was Matt. Always polite.

When Woll finally reached the sheriff's office in Van Buren, Arkansas, the manhunt began.

With some bravado, Matt had told Woll that he and his brother would never be taken alive, and to the posse out after them, "dead or alive" made little difference.

Officers who knew the Kimes family figured the boys would head for a relative's home near Rudy, Arkansas, and they pushed hard to get there before the two could hole up in the wooded hills surrounding the house. The

69

posse got there first, and settled down to wait. Hours passed, and eventually, the boys came. As they crossed a shallow creek and moved out of the shadows, the officers called out, "All right, boys, get your hands up!"

Both whirled back toward the creek, and the posse opened fire. One went down. A second volley caught the other. Both had flesh wounds, and following medical treatment, they were returned to the Oklahoma State Penitentiary for safekeeping. The warden is supposed to have greeted the brothers with "I told you to steer clear of Roy Brandon."

Trial was held in Sallisaw during August, 1926. Although they were tried for murder, the jury called it manslaughter and recommended twenty-five years imprisonment for George and thirty-five years for Matt. George accepted the sentence. Matt appealed, and in November, a judge reversed the manslaughter charge, called it murder, and ordered Matt to prison for life.

George's short-lived crime spree was finished, with one exception. As prisoner No. 16614, he escaped from the penitentiary on July 2, 1948, and was recaptured nearly a year later in Burns, Oregon, where he worked in a lumber camp under the name of Arnold Alford. He was returned to Oklahoma on June 14, 1949, and given No. 38167. In May, 1957, he walked out of prison a free man. He worked a short time on an Oklahoma ranch, then moved to Oregon to continue working in the logging camp.

Matt's crime spree was just beginning, however.

On the night of November 21, 1926, he escaped from the Sallisaw jail with the help of six men who swarmed into the third-story cell area with shotguns and revolvers ready. Before anyone in town could form a posse, the crooks were away in cars and into the nearby hill country.

This time Kimes made national headlines, something he seemed to enjoy. He'd finally made enough of an impact that he was right up there with Capone, Dillinger, Pretty Boy Floyd, and Baby Face Nelson, not to mention Jesse and Frank James. It was apparently during this time in 1926 and the first few months in 1927 that Kimes made his way to Borger, where his newfound reputation made him something of a hero to be admired — and feared. Since most of the early law officers in town were from Oklahoma they knew Kimes and apparently he knew them. Either way, he was on friendly terms with the law, and it wasn't uncommon to see him sitting in the Borger police station talking with members of the force. When things became particularly hot, Kimes always disappeared and as the Texas Rangers found in 1927, Kimes was tipped off about raids by the local constabulary. As a result, Kimes never spent a day in city or county jails in Borger.

In January, 1927, Kimes and his gang swooped down upon a small country bank in Oklahoma and made off with nearly $40,000. One of the gang members was Roy Brandon.

Then, Kimes tried to out-Jesse Jesse James by robbing the three banks in Beggs, Oklahoma, his hometown, one right after the other. On May 18, 1927, he and his cohorts hit the First National Bank, then went down the street to the Farmer's National. On their way to bank number three they ran into Police Chief W. J. McAnally. About that time, someone yelled that the banks had been robbed, and McAnally drew his pistol and jumped behind a telephone pole. Kimes and his gang jumped into two separate cars.

McAnally emptied his revolver into one fleeing car, but apparently never heard the second as it sped up behind him. He was hit by a shotgun blast and died within a couple of minutes.

The hunt for the robbers was intense. Ten miles out law enforcement officers found one of the cars smashed against a rock. In the back seat was a can of nitroglycerin mixed for easy explosion. A folding seat beside the driver had been removed and a machine gun mounted in its place.

Roy Brandon was the first picked up, and following intensive questioning, his brother Clyde was arrested. Another member, whose name was withheld, told police where they could find Kimes. They were told to look for him at the Grand Canyon about June 18.

He was five days late. Kimes' mother was seriously ill and Matt is said to have spent some time with her in Van Buren, Arkansas. It was while he was driving through Oklahoma on his way west that he was recognized. Pursuit proved futile as Matt took to the hills. He did, however, have to abandon his car and suitcases. On June 23, he arrived at the Grand Canyon and was immediately recognized by a park ranger registering visitors.

The sheriff at Flagstaff was called, and Kimes was located at the Bright Angel Cafe. His youthful appearance fooled the sheriff, however. Kimes, with a smile on his face, told the sheriff he'd been mistaken for "this Kimes fellow before." Even when the sheriff showed him a picture, the bank robber just shook his head and said, "That's not me."

But the sheriff said they would just go down to headquarters to straighten it all out, and Kimes agreed. He even offered the sheriff the use of his car. With the calm and debonair attitude of Kimes, the sheriff was lulled into thinking that he might have made a mistake, and that in itself was a mistake. Instead of stopping at the park headquarters, Kimes stomped his foot down on the gas and sped on by. The sheriff reacted quickly, and the struggle brought the car perilously close to the edge of the canyon. Kimes, fighting the sheriff off with one arm, suddenly stopped the car, pulled a .45 automatic and shot at the sheriff. He missed. Then, he grabbed the sheriff by the throat and choked him into unconsciousness.

Two park rangers had heard the shot and drove up

near the parked car. Kimes menaced them with his .45, and they backed off. Then, the bandit dropped over the canyon rim.

The Grand Canyon was not the Ozarks nor the Cookson Hills of Oklahoma. Five hours later Kimes surrendered. He was exhausted. By the time he was returned to Oklahoma, all members of the gang had been captured, and all were given speedy trials — courts did that sort of thing back in the '20s — with sentences ranging from twelve to twenty-five years.

Roy Brandon died a few months after imprisonment. Kimes was sentenced to death for the murder of McAnally, but this was changed to life. He became a "model" prisoner and worked toward a parole, and in July, 1945, following several years of doing what he was told, he was given two months' freedom as a test of his sincerity. His release was to be an embarrassment to Governor Robert Kerr and the prison warden.

Kimes did so well during the two months he was out that the governor extended his freedom to six months. On November 17, 1945, Kimes made headlines again. He robbed the Morton, Texas, bank, taking $17,000. The hunt took officers all over Oklahoma and throughout Texas. He was seen everywhere, sometimes miles apart by informants.

Then the search centered in Arkansas, when, on a wet, fog-ridden night of December 1, 1945, young Joe Chamblee, a truck driver, hit a man who had stepped out from between two cars. Chamblee tried to stop, but couldn't, and the badly injured man was taken to a Little Rock hospital. He was registered in as Leo A. Woods of Miami, Oklahoma.

Doctors spent hours taking stitches and setting a badly broken leg. The man complained of head and abdominal pains. He didn't want his family informed, and that bothered hospital officials. They became more upset when they found $1,600 in Woods' wallet and a pistol in his overcoat. They called police and after some sharp

detective work, they came up with the man's real name
— Matthew Edward Kimes!

On December 13, Kimes' condition worsened and a last resort operation was done. At 8 a.m. on December 14, Kimes died, not the victim of a wild shoot-out with police, but from being run over by a chicken truck.

Few, if any, mourned his death in Borger.

TEXAS RANGERS POSE with Borger jail residents, 1926. The criminals are connected together on a chain called the trot line.

Photo courtesy of the Hutchinson County Historical Commission.

75

5

Death Was No Stranger

Violent death was becoming all too familiar to the citizens of Borger. Enough so that Governor Dan Moody began getting lengthy letters from disturbed businessmen and residents who wanted him to declare martial law to put an end to the indiscriminate killings, hijackings, bootlegging, prostitution, and general corruption.

Texas Ranger Captain Frank Hamer said that Borger's bad reputation inspired some bad poetry from one citizen who left the town for a safer home. It began:

> *Let's sing a song of Borger,*
> *Famed for its graft and rot.*
> *It's just a wide place in the wood,*
> *This town that God forgot,*
> *For this village large boasts deeper sin,*
> *Than Sodom ever knew;*
> *Come lend an ear, kind stranger,*
> *And I'll whisper them to you . . . .*

The first recorded murder was that of M.F. McWilliams, about twenty-eight, who was shot on November 30, 1926, and who died on December 2. The list of killings, some said to be out-and-out assassinations, grew —

- Dec. 19, 1926: John C. Campbell, a holdup man, killed by night officer, gunshot wounds.
- Dec. 22, 1926: Roy Martin, gunshot wound in head, man found dead five miles west of Borger.
- Jan. 15, 1927: Mrs. Edna Monte, housewife, born July 7, 1893, in Wisconsin, killed at filling station in Whittenburg during holdup; pistol wound in chest. Buried in New London, Wisconsin.
- Jan. 10, 1927: Paul Evans, born Oct. 14, 1894, field superintendent, Grover Corp., a firm erecting steel towers. Killed two and a half miles southwest of Borger. A homicide.
- Jan. 28, 1927: Benito Medina, about thirty-five, a laborer, found dead, three and a half miles northeast of Borger. Death due to cerebral hemorrhage.
- Feb. 1, 1927: Harry Valentine, about thirty, killed in dance hall in Borger. A homicide.
- March 19, 1927: Coke Buchanan, about fifty-three, a police officer, of gunshot on Dixon Street, a homicide. Buried in Waco, Tex.
- March 26, 1927: William Parks, about forty, a driller, died of gunshot wounds in Stinnett.
- March 26, 1927: W.M. Parks, born Feb. 12, 1886, cafe owner, shot and killed in Stinnett.

(NOTE: Although the record shows Parks was a driller, it is quite probable that William Parks and W.M. Parks are the same person. The age fits.)

- April 1, 1927: A.L. Terry, born June 8, 1882, police officer, of gunshot wounds, one mile north of Borger.
- April 1, 1927: D.P. Kenyon, about forty-five, police officer, of gunshot wounds, one mile north of Borger. Buried in Kaw City, Okla.

77

(NOTE: There are strong indications that the killing of these two police officers were deliberate assassinations.)

- April 13, 1927: Earnest Edward Dane, born Oct. 16, 1898, nitroglycerin explosion, death instantaneous.
- May 7, 1927: Claud Miller Hays, an oilworker, born July 4, 1896, of gunshot wounds.
- May 19, 1927: George E. Norsworthy, born Jan. 13, 1903, a miner, of gunshot wounds.

Life in Borger for the "decent folk" was becoming intolerable. The Borger law was ineffective (and generally corrupt) and the legitimate businessmen took their complaints about the breakdown in law enforcement to Governor Moody.

On April 4, 1927, Governor Moody sent Frank A. Hamer, Captain of Company D, to investigate conditions in Borger. Within two days, Hamer told the governor that "the worst crime ring I have seen in my twenty-three years as an officer exists in Borger." Hamer asked for additional Rangers, much to the consternation of the city's newspaper, chamber of commerce, and local politicos. They all protested against Moody's decision to send in the Rangers.

On April 8, the governor sent a wire to Marvin Thomas, secretary of the Borger Chamber of Commerce:

Your wire the sixth period Vehement protests will not prevent declaration of martial law period Reports reaching me from investigations made at my direction by persons in whom I have confidence tell of a condition of open law violation that is not to be tolerated period Local enforcement officers have not discharged their duties period The way to prevent martial law is

*to bring about immediate correction of condi-
tions period This can best be accomplished by
removal of law enforcement officers who have
not discharged their duties and replacing them
with men who will see to enforcement of the law
period*

Moody also informed Mayor John R. Miller that it
was the governor's "constitutional duty to cause the
laws to be faithfully executed" and that the "power exists to carry out this duty" and that as governor, he
knew when and how to use that power.

Miller got the message, and on April 18, he and Commissioners W.T. Malone and Glenn A. Pace sent a letter
to Moody expressing their "sincere appreciation for your
actions in giving to us your assistance in adjusting local
conditions here with reference to lawlessness." They also
hedged on their inability to control the situation by telling Moody that "owing to the fact that our City has
grown too rapidly during the past twelve months and
with no money available to properly operate the City affairs which were necessary to avoid such conditions as
existed, we trust you feel that we have done everything
within our power to avoid such." In the light of what was
to come in the near future, this had to be one of the most
hypocritical letters sent by the city's governmental
body. The one thing they didn't want was too deep a
probe into the city's affairs.

Moody didn't buy it anyway. Following Hamer's request for additional Rangers, he assigned Captain Tom
Hickman, Company B; Captain William W. Sterling,
Company D; Sergeant W.W. Taylor, Company C;
Privates Hardy B. Purvis, Company B and Jim E. Mc-
Coy, Headquarters Company, plus three others to clean
up the city. They were to stay in Borger "until the
lawless unconditionally surrender," and in the tradition
of the Old West, they gave the outlaws "until sundown"
to clear out.

Sterling, who had been appointed captain of Company B, then stationed in Del Rio, on April 15, arrived in Borger on April 17. When asked by newsmen what tactics the Rangers would use, he said they were "simply going to reverse the customary Borger procedure. Where the criminals had been killing officers, we were going to kill off some of the crooks."

The statement had the psychological effect it was supposed to have. The Rangers didn't have to shoot anyone, but then few of the crooks stuck around long enough to see whether the Rangers meant it or not. As Sterling observed, the crooks "were strung out along the highways in droves, some in cars and trucks, others afoot. Outbound trains, both passenger and freight, also did a land office business in transporting these undesirables."

More than 200 vice arrests were made. Liquor traffic was broken up, several stills were destroyed, and thousands of gallons of rotgut whiskey were poured onto the ground. Some 203 slot machines were broken into pieces with sledge hammers and axes. Many spectators watched the one-armed bandits being destroyed, and men would step out occasionally and ask to help, saying they had always wanted to beat one of the mechanical hijackers, and this was about the only way it could be done. Money from the nickel and quarter machines was turned over to the Salvation Army.

Numerous gambling resorts were placed under surveillance and forced to close or clean up. Several "emergency hospitals" were closed down. These weren't hospitals in the accepted sense, but were run by defrocked doctors or those with questionable credentials. Some of the "doctors" had been run out of other towns because of their penchant for prescribing narcotics. Sterling found that "these quacks would construct large, barn-like buildings out of cheap lumber, cut them up into small rooms and recruit some "nurses" of the same stripe ... The unfortunate who fell into their clutches should have been called victims instead of patients. Many complaints were received from injured men who had been thrown out of these places after being robbed of their valuables."

An estimated 1,200 prostitutes left town, and many of the cleaning and pressing firms reported that they had several hundred gaudy silk dresses on hand which had been left by their owners. The Rangers suggested that the dresses be given to the Salvation Army.

The cleanup pleased some; displeased others.

O.C. Goodwin of Sno-White Stores Company, Inc., a Texas corporation whose slogan was *"where cleanliness reigns supreme,"* wrote the governor that "there are many good decent people in Borger who are glad the Rangers are here, and we want you to keep them here until this bunch of outlaws has left town or surrendered. Most of these good, decent businessmen are afraid to come out in the open and take a stand here as they would like to do for fear that some of these thugs will shoot them in the back some dark night.

"The Chamber of Commerce here has so utterly failed to function as it should — which is 'to do the most good for the most people' — that a few of us got together recently and organized the Borger Commercial Club, of which organization I was made President, and we are making some headway. This morning an article appeared in the *Amarillo News* to the effect that the newspaperman of Borger called Homer D. Wade, manager of the West Texas C. of C., over the phone and solicited his aid in getting the Rangers removed from Borger, and that Wade promised he would intercede with you to that end. I immediately called some of our men into a little meeting to discuss the situation. We then had a meeting with Ranger Captains Hickman and Hamer, offering them our support and cooperation.

"Some of us know the real situation and feel that it will be a sad day for the good people here if the Rangers are withdrawn at this time. We feel that the thing you should do is to declare 'martial law' at once and clean up things right, and it will take some time to do so then. The crooks here must be starved out or run out of town, and you can't do this in a week or two."

Pressure from the Rangers forced Miller and the commissioners to resign along with the chief of police and nearly all of the police force. Glenn Pace, one of the commissioners, was elected mayor and J.E. Higgins and W.E. Karns became commissioners. Pace was a poor choice, but then this wasn't learned until later.

Not only did some of the minor characters of Borger's underworld leave, but some major ones as well. Notable among them were J. William (Whitey) Walker, Matt Kimes, Ace Pendleton, Ed Bailey, and Ray Terrell.

Walker, a member of Oklahoma's infamous Cotton Top Walker Gang, was in jail when the Rangers arrived. He had been locked up on April 1, 1927, along with his brother, Hugh, and Ed Bailey for the March 19 shooting of Coke Buchanan. The Dixon Creek police officer died with six bullets in him during a battle with five men when he went to the aid of a fellow officer, Sam Williams, who was being beaten with pistols.

All three were released on $7,500 bond each — Hugh on April 19; Bailey, April 28; and Walker, May 14. As soon as Whitey got out, all three skipped town. On the day of his disappearance, Whitey sent a note to the *Borger Herald* saying, "I am leaving for awhile until I can get a fair trial. I don't want to be the goat of a frameup." He also said that he had "always played fair."

Whitey and Pendleton, wanted for masterminding the Pampa bank robbery, teamed up to rob banks in Wyoming, New Mexico, Colorado, Oklahoma, Texas, Arkansas, and Louisiana. With them part of the time were Owen Edwards, the alleged killer of police officers Terry and Kenyon; Fred Nave, a dance hall operator in Borger and killer of Jack Morgan of Childress, Texas, and Clayton Tontz, a Borger hijacker and friend of Walker's. Tontz is said to have killed John Langley, an

Amarillo druggist, during a hijacking, but the case was dismissed for lack of evidence.

On September 19, 1928, Whitey, Clayton, Tontz, and Edwards robbed the bank at Covington, Oklahoma, getting away with $20,000. There was a running gun battle with police; however, the bandits escaped. The next day Tontz' body was found near Stroud, Oklahoma. He had been shot through the heart by his "friend" Whitey for his $5,000 share of the loot. The police report showed that Tontz' coat was "neatly folded under his head."

About six weeks later, Edwards was killed in a gunfight with officers at Harjo, Oklahoma, a town about twenty-five miles from Seminole, following a bank robbery. Police Officer Jim Kiersey died in that shoot-out.

Whitey and Pendleton, by this time, were wanted in nearly every state in the Southwest, and the search for both became nationwide. Rewards totaling $50,000 were offered for their arrest. On January 15, 1929, Whitey and Fred Nave were arrested in Buffalo, New York, by Detective Sergeant McCarty, who recognized both of them from photos on unwanted posters. The two men were well dressed and wore expensive jewelry. McCarty told Hutchinson County Sheriff Joe Ownbey that "their whiskers, which they had grown for a disguise, attracted my attention."

Whitey and Nave had given fictitious names and had said they had arrived in Buffalo in their private airplane and were leaving for Florida shortly. Whitey told McCarty his name was Clyde Roberts.

McCarty took the two men to police headquarters, fingerprinted both and put their photos on the wire. Captain Frank Hamer telegraphed McCarty that both men were escape artists and to watch them closely. He did. A policeman with a tear gas bomb and sawed-off shotgun sat in front of their cells. Another, similarly armed, was stationed outside the locked door of the cell room, while a third stood guard on the ground floor of the police station.

Meanwhile, the police at Colorado Springs, Colorado, wired McCarty that "Roberts' " real name was Byron Walker (it wasn't) and that he personally was responsible for the murder of a bank president, the president's son, a bank teller and a physician during a bank holdup at Lamar, Colorado, in May, 1928. Police Chief H. D. Harper said Byron Walker led the band of bandits that robbed the First National Bank of Lamar on May 23, 1928, of $11,000 cash, $8,000 in Liberty Bonds, and $200,000 in other securities.

"Walker is one of the most desperate men in the country," the chief wired. "Our chase for him has led us through New Mexico, Oklahoma, Texas, and on to Buffalo. He headed a gang of robbers that killed three officers in Borger in 1927, and his band of killers and robbers was made up of remnants of the Ray Terrell gang that has terrorized Kansas and Oklahoma and the Ace Pendleton band that operated in the West for several years."

Chief Harper was confused, although at the time he wasn't aware of it, and he didn't learn of his error until he discovered that Whitey had an alibi for the time of the May 23 robbery in Lamar. Harper and Sheriff Fred Bowles of Ada, Oklahoma, traveled to Buffalo to pick up the two outlaws. Whitey was wanted for murder, but Nave, at that time, was wanted only for liquor violations and jumping $500 bond in Pampa. Twelve detectives helped Chief Harper and Sheriff Bowles put the two on the train for Colorado.

However, when Harper learned of his mistake, the two outlaws were released to Texas authorities to stand trial. It was found later that George J. Abshier, Howard L. Royston, and Ralph Fleagle robbed the Lamar bank and cold-bloodedly killed the four men. Colorado Governor W. H. Adams ordered Walker and Nave turned over to Texas officials following a two-day extradition hearing. Oklahoma officers wanted Walker for bank robbery at Nardin, Oklahoma, and several other states wanted him, but it was Texas who got him.

Clem Calhoun, appointed district attorney following Johnny Holmes' assassination, wrote Governor Moody that "we do not have any case at all against Whitey Walker that we can expect to get a conviction in. Judge Pickens and Judge Willis both concur in this belief. Sheriff Fred Bowles of Ada, Oklahoma, is here now for Walker. From all the information I can gather they have the best case against him. I understand that Bell County, Texas, (Whitey's home county) has filed a protest against him going to Oklahoma. I further understand that the Bell County case is only for burglary which carries a small term or penalty.

"Walker intimated to me that he would plead guilty here if I would recommend a small term in pen but sufficiently long to give the Oklahoma cases time to die and pass away. I am sure that Walker would plead guilty in Bell County in order to keep away from Oklahoma. I never saw a man as completely unnerved as Walker was when the Oklahoma Sheriff walked in the jail to see him. His whole conduct proved to me that he is telling the truth when he says he does not want to go to Oklahoma and will not go if possible."

Walker was in the Stinnett jail from October 1, 1929, to November 4, 1929. That was the day he tried to escape.

Believing that he was being taken to another county for safekeeping from some rather irate Hutchinson County citizens, Whitey told his brother Hugh he "was going to Dallas, I expect."

Texas Ranger W.H. Kirby and Sheriff C.O. Moore took Whitey about two miles toward Borger, where, to Walker's surprise, Oklahoma officers were waiting for him. When he was told he was going to Oklahoma, Whitey yelled, "I'll be damned if I do," and tried to leap out of the car. He didn't make it. He was transferred to a second car with Sheriff Bowles and one of his deputies inside. Both carried rifles and machine guns. Walker, they determined, wasn't going to get away this time.

It's understandable that Walker didn't want to return to Oklahoma. There were too many charges against him. He had robbed the banks at Purcell, Newkirk, Lamont, Nardin, Prague, and the First National at Allen, to name a few. If he had had his "rathers," he would take the maximum sentence of twelve years for a jewelry store robbery in Bell County. He knew that his partner, Curtis Black, in the Allen bank robbery had gotten ninety-nine years, and Whitey expected at least that or the electric chair. Following trial in Oklahoma, he was sentenced to the penitentiary at McAlester for ninety-nine years.

Meanwhile, the charge of murder against Hugh Walker for the killing of Coke Buchanan was dismissed for "lack of evidence." Hugh moved to Lubbock, where he opened a gambling hall. He shot Frank V. Brown because Brown refused to return $1,000 he had won in Hugh's place. Walker was sent to Huntsville for ninety-nine years, but was released within three years.

The saga of his brother, Whitey, wasn't finished, however.

On August 30, 1933, he, Roy Johnson, and W.D. Peoples (alias Irvin Thompson alias Blackie Thompson) escaped from the Oklahoma pen. Shortly thereafter a jewelry store in Bryan, Texas, was robbed, then a bank at Buckholts and another at Palestine. They got $41,000 from the First State Bank at Marlin, Texas.

A nationwide hunt was started for the men, and on January 26, 1934, Police Inspector Frank Mitchell of Miami, Florida, arrested Peoples. On January 29, Whitey and Johnson were captured in Tallahassee, Florida, following a battle with police. Both of the outlaws were wounded.

All three were returned to Texas for trial in Marlin. Walker, TDC #76454, arrived in Huntsville on June 4,

1934, to serve a sentence of ninety-nine years for robbery by firearms. Johnson, Texas Department of Corrections #75689, arrived in Huntsville on March 14, 1934, following conviction in Brazos County for robbery by firearms. He received a sentence of ninety-nine years, but was granted a conditional pardon and placed in custody of the Oklahoma State Penitentiary on April 2, 1945. Blackie Thompson TDC #75862, arrived in Huntsville on March 31, 1933, convicted of robbery by firearms. His sentence was ninety-nine years.

On July 22, 1934, Walker, Blackie Thompson, Ray Hamilton, Joe Palmer, and Charlie Frazier, a lifer and accomplice of Thompson's, made a break for freedom. Frazier was shot off a ladder by a prison guard. Walker was killed. Palmer, Thompson, and Hamilton made it safely over the wall.

On December 5, 1934, Thompson was killed near the outskirts of Amarillo in a three-minute shoot-out with police and sheriff's deputies.

One final word about Ray Terrell and Ace Pendleton.

Although Matt Kimes and Ray Terrell were regarded as a matched pair, and were supposed to have made up the Kimes-Terrell gang, Terrell himself said he and Kimes never worked together. Kimes, Terrell said, was a daylight stickup man, something he couldn't do. Terrell opened bank vaults at night with electric or acetylene torches. Once the Rangers came into town in 1927, the two men headed for Oklahoma and other states to continue their bank robberies.

Terrell, said to be a protege of Al Spencer, a noted border bandit, was, as was Kimes, born in the shadow of the Cookson Hills, the rendezvous of innumerable fugitives during Oklahoma's territorial days. Terrell had a criminal record that would have compared favorably with any of the old-time bandits moving down the Owl Hoot Trail. He was a master bank robber, and when Spencer was killed in the Osage Hills by a posse headed by U.S. Marshal Alva McDonald, Terrell became head of his own gang.

His area of operation was Oklahoma and Arkansas, and he became one of the most wanted men of the time. He was arrested in early 1926 for robbing the bank at Pawnee, Oklahoma, but he sawed his way out of jail and went to robbing banks a few days later. He was caught six months later following the robbery of the bank at Ardmore, Oklahoma, and again, he sawed his way out of jail.

Terrell disappeared for several months. Then, he was surprised in a farm house near Joplin, Missouri, and arrested. Handcuffed to Sheriff John Johnston of Sallisaw, Oklahoma, and accompanied by Lee Pollock, a member of the Oklahoma Bureau of Investigation, Terrell was started back to Oklahoma to stand trial for his numerous crimes.

They were practically within the shadow of the prison walls at McAlester, when Terrell slipped out of the handcuffs, leaped from the car into the darkness, and disappeared, an event that was an embarrassment to both law officers.

Terrell was heard of again in April, 1927, when the Hillsboro, Texas, sheriff's department got a tip that Terrell might make an attempt to free his wife, jailed for assisting in the robbery of jewelry stores in Hillsboro and Temple, Texas. Extra deputies were sworn in, and a small arsenal installed in the Hill County jail.

Mrs. Terrell, apparently unperturbed by it all, observed to her jailers that her husband had gotten her out of jail three times before, and she saw no reason why he wouldn't get her out again. She was wrong. Her husband never showed up.

He finally was captured and sentenced to twenty-five years in prison. In 1936, he was released and he opened a cafe, apparently leading a decent life from then on.

Pendleton, jailed in Eldorado, Arkansas, was asked to be returned to Gray County, Texas, by Sheriff E.S. Graves, but the bank robber was sent to Okemah, Oklahoma, instead. He died there of tuberculosis.

By June, 1927, the Rangers felt they had done a fairly decent cleanup job in Borger. City officials had been changed. Most of the major criminal element had moved out, and the town was beginning to settle down.

However, M.T. Gonzaullas, winding up an investigation as a Federal Prohibition Agent, wrote A.B. Butler, assistant prohibition administrator, Fort Worth, Texas:

> Per your instructions of May 5, 1927, I conducted a special investigation of Hutchinson County officials, Borger City officials and illicit liquor ring operating in Borger and Hutchinson County. This investigation was carried forward with the cooperation and assistance of the Texas Ranger Force.
>
> I wish to report, after thorough investigation of the above matter, that there was a conspiracy existing between the Hutchinson County officials, Borger city officials, and illicit liquor ring, illegal gambling ring, organized vice operating houses of prostitution, and criminal activity in general at Borger, and in Hutchinson County. At the time the Texas Rangers opened up their cleanup campaign in Borger they broke up this conspiracy and ring and forced most of them to leave this section of the country. However, there are still in this community a number of leaders of this ring, who have remained and are holding public office as Borger City Officials and Hutchinson County Officials, but there is no conspiracy now existing; I wish to add that I questioned numerous persons who advised me of the above conspiracy, but could not testify from their

own knowledge; and all persons that would have been material witnesses for the United States Government and the State of Texas in the prosecution of the above ring have left this section of the country, their whereabouts unknown. These persons left during the cleanup campaign, most of them being violators themselves who were advised to leave this community by the Texas Rangers; others, who were not criminals, left for fear of being molested by the members of the ring for having given information.

It is my opinion that it is not now possible to make a conspiracy case against the above ring, but it is my further opinion that if the remaining members of the ring, now holding official positions, are not closely watched they will reorganize and a conspiracy will exist and conditions in Borger and Hutchinson County will be the same as they were previous to the Texas Ranger's cleanup campaign.

Although the murders in Borger slowed down during the Ranger cleanup, they began again shortly following the departure of the Ranger force.

- June 18, 1928: Blane Crider, forty-six, oilworker, bullet wound in heart.
- Sept. 10, 1928: Frank Ragan, farmer, violence to head and blood clot on the brain.
- Sept. 11, 1928: Harry E. Losey, merchant, born March 7, 1888 in Nebraska; gunshot wound in abdomen.
- Nov. 20, 1928: Hattie Richardson, born 1904; single, black; died from gunshot wound; shot by C.C. Carter.
- Feb. 2, 1929: Joe T. Hutson, city policeman

born March 12, 1889, of accidental gunshot wound.

- Feb. 16, 1929: Charles Goff, cook, born June 10, 1885; gunshot wounds, death within thirty minutes.
- April 15, 1929: Mrs. Mae Turner, born June 30, 1893, from gunshot wounds; a homicide.
- Aug. 18, 1929: Homer Brown, born Dec. 27, 1906, a laborer; wounds inflicted by knife.
- Sept. 5, 1929: A.A. Ray, about forty-five, died of cerebral hemorrhage caused by shock, fall, or blow on head.
- Sept. 13, 1929: John A. Holmes, born Jan. 20, 1886, in Mississippi; father — T.S. Holmes, born in Durant, Mississippi; mother — Mary Ella Salus, born in Salus, Mississippi; died from gunshot wounds inflicted by person or persons unknown. Inquest held September 13 by Walter S. Broomhall, Jr.; burial Sept. 17, 1929 in Panhandle, Texas, Wilson-Buntin Undertakers.
- Sept. 15, 1929: Melvin Hotchkiss, born April 12, 1903, trucker, of knife wound of left leg, inflicted by person or persons unknown.

When Governor Dan Moody received word that Holmes had been killed, his patience with Borger ended, and he sent ten Rangers back to Borger and called out the Texas National Guard.

6

Martial Law

Declaring martial law was not without precedent. Governors prior to Moody had done so when local authorities "did not enforce the law, suppress the insurrections and disorderly conduct, and compel obedience to law, or where they aid and encourage the lawless element." Borger certainly met the latter criteria.

In June, 1919, Governor William P. Hobby (August 25, 1917-January 18, 1921) sent a detachment of the Texas National Guard, commanded by Brigadier General Robert H. McDill, and Texas Rangers, commanded by Captain Joe Brooks, to police the town of Longview, troubled by a race riot. Martial law lasted ten days, during which time twenty-six white men and several peace officers were arrested.

The Guard was called out a second time during September, 1919, when a hurricane destroyed a considerable amount of property in Corpus Christi, Aransas Pass, Rockport, and Port Aransas. Governor Hobby sent both infantry and cavalry troops into the area to guard property exposed by the storm. They were to "aid in the recovery of bodies of the dead; to recover property which had been carried by the storm waters to various sections of the low lying shore along Nueces and Aransas Bays; to help rebuild bridges, public roads, railroad lines, and telephone and telegraph lines; to direct the burning of dead carcasses of cattle, horses, mules, hogs, or snakes, and to kill rattlesnakes that had been brought by the waters from St. Joe Island; to direct the clearing away of debris, consisting of destroyed business houses and dwellings, of trunks of trees and other material that had been washed ashore; to supervise the receipt and distribution of supplies for relief purposes."

The civil authorities in this instance cooperated fully with the military. The Guard remained in Corpus for thirty days, and as Brigadier General Jacob Wolters, commanding officer, observed, "It was hard, disagreeable work for soldiers."

Governor Hobby called out the Guard on June 7, 1920, when rioting began and shots were fired during a strike among employees on the Mallory and Morgan Line docks in Galveston. The workers were members of the International Longshoremen's Association, and those employed by Mallory were white, mostly of foreign birth, though naturalized citizens, while the workers at the Morgan docks were Negro. The total number of strikers was about 1,600.

Pickets, armed with clubs, prevented anyone from approaching the Mallory or Morgan docks, and the records are filled with assaults committed by Negroes and white strikers on white men.

Wolters, commanding the Guard, said the "police were sympathetic with the strikers and did not interfere with these assaults. When they did make arrests, it was invariably the assaulted victim who found himself arrested and charged with vagrancy. It was a real organized, armed insurrection."

By the time marial law ended in Galveston, October 7, 1920, 954 arrests had been made.

Governor Pat M. Neff (January 18, 1921-January 20, 1925) proclaimed martial law in Mexia on January 11, 1922, after twenty Rangers and six prohibition agents found they were unable to stop the murders, highway

STANDING BEFORE THE Adobe Walls Monument in the Texas Panhandle during the first Borger cleanup are, standing left to right, Wesley Bryce, Capt. W.W. Sterling and Capt. Frank A. Hamer. Seated, Deputy Sheriff Jack DeGraftenreid and Ranger Hardy Purvis.

(Photo from Trails and Trials of a Texas Ranger, William W. Sterling. University of Oklahoma Press, 1968.)

robberies, gambling, bootlegging, and prostitution in the booming oil town. Wolters again was in command of the Guard.

Mexia, an average, quiet, morally clean town of approximately 2,500 inhabitants, grew suddenly into a town of 30,000, with the discovery of oil. The sheriff hired deputies "who had had the experience" in other oil fields. The town marshal employed the same class of people as policemen. When these "law enforcement" officials were questioned about the activities in town, they expressed shock and amazement that anything was going on. Not far from Mexia was the Chicken Farm, a well known house of prostitution, built on land sold to the operator by a deputy sheriff and within 200 yards of the deputy's residence.

Martial law finally ended in Mexia at the end of February, 1922.

With the exception of quelling another strike (Denison, Texas, July 26-October 21, 1922), the state was relatively quiet until Governor Dan Moody (January 17, 1927-January 20, 1931) proclaimed martial law in Borger.

Moody called the murder of District Attorney Johnny Holmes "a dastardly crime of a low-life assassin," and "one of the worst crimes ever committed in Texas." Moody, who had been attorney general of Texas prior to becoming governor, made it clear that the killer of his friend would be prosecuted right into the death chamber. "I shall employ the best lawyers I can find and shall ask that he be given the death penalty if Texas juries have one left."

In a letter to E.A. Simpson, an Amarillo attorney, Moody said, "This case is one of the gravest law violations that has occurred in this State within my memory. It is an instance in which organized crime has raised its head not only to defy the law, but to take the life of one charged with the public responsibility of enforcing the law. A statement of the circumstances shows that the crime was deliberately planned and executed in a most cowardly and heartless manner."

Moody put up $500 of his own money as a reward for information leading to the conviction of Holmes' murderer. The Texas County and District Attorneys Association, through its president, William McCraw of Dallas, added another $250. Borger's citizens also began accumulating reward money, which eventually amounted to several thousands of dollars.

In addition to the reward money, McCraw sent a telegram to Moody, stating, "I am sending Nash Adams, my assistant, and Mr. Grady Kennedy, special investigator, to Borger to assist the Rangers in the investigation of the murder of District Attorney Holmes and feel that as president of the County Attorneys Association this will be warranted."

Moody called in Brigadier General Jacob F. Wolters, now an old hand at taming recalcitrant boom towns. Wolters, a balding, burly man in his late fifties, "was a good lawyer, but a politician whose success had never matched his ambition; he had won election to county attorney and state representative, but had lost a race for the U.S. Senate. He loved both the law and the military. He had been a first lieutenant in the Texas cavalry unit he had helped organize during the Spanish-American War, but he didn't get overseas." His experience in putting down strikes, race riots, and the handling the lawless conditions in new oil areas was what Moody needed to control the situation in Borger.

As if to confirm in his own mind what he had already decided to do, Moody asked Wolters if he would declare martial law if he were governor. Wolters, sensing that that is just what Moody wanted to do, said he would, and the governor told the general to muster his troops and get them into Borger as soon as possible. "Keep your preparations secret, and tell your men to do the same," Moody ordered.

Under confidential cover, Wolters wrote to Colonels

L.E. McGee and Louis S. Davidson, commanding officers of the 112th and 124th Cavalry, respectively. These two regiments were part of the 56th Cavalry Brigade. They were to select twelve officers and eighty enlisted men from Headquarters Troop, Troops A, B, and E, 112th Cavalry, and Troops A and B, 124th Cavalry, and an officer and four men from the Medical Detachment, 112th Cavalry.

Wolters wanted enlisted men "who had served not less than eighteen months with their unit; who were unmarried, who had no dependents and who were dependable young men both in military and civil life." He also wanted a greater percent of non-commissioned officers than would be used ordinarily in so small a detachment.

He cautioned his officers that "whatever was done must be carried on so secretly that no inkling of it would break to the public." Newspapermen throughout the state knew, however, that something was up. Rumors and the "no comments" from the governor's office were enough to keep reporters digging away, watching for any unusual activity.

The sequence of events which culminated with the arrival of troops in Borger were these:

Shortly following Holmes' murder, Governor Moody was in Houston and told General Wolters "it might become necessary to declare martial law in Hutchinson County."

Wolters, told that he would be in command, wrote to the commanding officers of the 112th and 124th Cavalry, outlining briefly what he wanted done. His instructions were to "select officers whose efficiency were well established, and who could afford to leave their avocations or jobs for an indefinite period."

The troop commanders called in the officers they had selected and briefed them, and helped select the enlisted men. Then the captains sent for the individual men and told them that there was to be a competitive mobilization test of detachments selected from the

Dallas and Fort Worth troops, and that the Dallas detachment would be bussed to the armory of Troop A, 112th Cavalry at Fort Worth for additional competition.

Each man was instructed to draw regulation field equipment.

On September 21, 1929, eight days following Holmes' death, Wolters submitted his list of men to the Adjutant General, together with plans for mobilization. He requested two automobiles, two trucks and two ambulances be taken to Fort Worth during the night preceding "M Day." He also wanted a truck with 100 cots and other equipment to be driven from Camp Wolters at Mineral Wells to Fort Worth.

"M Day" was scheduled for 9 a.m., Sunday, September 29, 1929.

On September 25, Wolters visited Borger. Newsmen hounded him, trying to ascertain what the governor's decision was concerning martial law, and when the troops would move. Wolters passed the buck to the governor, whose office had no comment.

Wolters returned to Houston and his home on September 27, and on September 28, he and his adjutant, Captain Fred W. Edmiston, prepared General Orders 1, 2, and 3. Newsmen once again called repeatedly.

On September 28, Wolters left for Fort Worth dressed in civilian clothes.

At 6 p.m., Saturday, September 28, the Dallas soldiers were mobilized and they left the city for the armory at Fort Worth, reaching there about 9 p.m. They were told the officers would arrive on Sunday morning to judge the various competitions.

Sunday, September 29, saw competitive drills and minor problems being worked by the men. Mess was served at noon, and at 2 p.m., a train consisting of baggage car and three Pullmans moved onto a track near the armory. The men were formed and told to board the railcars. They were told they were going to an unnamed destination for an indefinite tour of duty, and that their families and employers would be notified the next day. The soldiers knew then they were headed for Borger.

The train moved around Fort Worth to the railyard where the freight cars with the motor transports were located. At 3 p.m. the train started on its trip to Borger, 400 miles away.

Wolters almost got away with it. No newsmen were around when the train left Fort Worth, but when the train arrived in Wichita Falls late that afternoon, one newspaperman was there. He asked the soldiers where they were headed, and they answered they did not know. Frustrated, the reporter asked, "Are you fellows all dummies?" And you know how soldiers are, they yelled out, "We sure are!"

The train arrived in Amarillo at 4 a.m., Monday, September 30, and was transferred to the Santa Fe station where it remained while breakfast was served. The men put on their uniforms. At 8:30 a.m., the train arrived in Borger.

Wolters wrote later that with ten Texas Rangers already in Borger he did not hesitate to have the train move directly to the depot. "I did not anticipate any hostile demonstrations and while a crowd of people had gathered at the station there was no demonstration one way or the other. The soldiers were detrained in an orderly manner on the side of each car, without word of command, with the rifle at port arms. Twenty-five paces in advance of each platoon were two selected men with riot shotguns at port arms.

"In every situation where military authority is used to aid the civil power things occur that have either a good or a bad psychological effect. They are, in common parlance, the 'breaks' of the game. We had just such a break at Borger. Within one minute after the troops had detrained, a drunk man approached one of the guards. He was promptly put under arrest. This occurrence, in the presence of spectators, had a good psychological effect, however minor the incident was."

Things happened quickly after that. A detachment of officers and men proceeded to city hall, where they disarmed members of the police force and constables and took possession of the offices and jail.

MPs were stationed at all city street intersections and patrols sent out throughout the city.

Another detachment of soldiers and Texas Rangers drove to Stinnett and declared martial law there, disarming all sheriff's department personnel.

Also, photostatic copies of the Governor's Proclamation and General Orders 1, 2, and 3 were posted throughout both cities.

The Governor's Proclamation in full was:

Proclamation
by the Governor
of the State of Texas

To all to whom these presents shall come:

WHEREAS, persons sent to Borger and Hutchinson County, Texas to investigate the situation regarding law enforcement have reported to me that:

there exists an organized and entrenched criminal ring in the City of Borger and in Hutchinson County; and that

the law in said city and county is not being effectively enforced by the existing law enforcing agencies, which is the fault not of the judiciary of the county, but of the peace officers of said city and county; and that

said peace officers are, for some reason, failing to suppress crime and bring criminals to justice; and that

at the present time without the presence of protecting authority, the responsible citizens of the community are intimidated and living under a menace which prevents them from informing on law violators; and that

at least one ex-convict is a peace officer in the county, and other peace officers have been charged with offenses of the grade of felony; and that

those who have been in said locality and reported to me have reported, first, that there is a conspiracy between the officers and the law violators and that affidavits have been secured to the passing of money to peace officers for protection from the enforcement of the law; and second, that witnesses who have been questioned concerning law violations, including the assassination of the District Attorney, have been threatened and driven from the county; and

WHEREAS, this condition has heretofore caused acts of violence on citizens of this State, and there is now imminent danger of insurrection, tumult, riot and breach of the peace, and serious danger to the inhabitants and property of citizens in the territory heretofore described; and

WHEREAS, Section 10 of Article 4 of the Constitution of Texas makes it the duty of the Governor of this State to "Cause the laws to be faithfully executed;" and

WHEREAS, Section 7 of Article 4 of the Constitution of Texas makes the Governor of this State the Commander-in-Chief of the military forces of this State, and gives him the "power to call forth the militia to execute the laws of the State."

NOW, THEREFORE, I, DAN MOODY, GOVERNOR OF TEXAS, and Commander-in-Chief of the military forces of this State, do by virtue of the authority vested in me under the Constitution and laws of this State, declare that the conditions above described do exist and are clearly violative of the Constitution and laws of this State, and that by reason of this the conditions contemplated in Article 5889 of the Revised Civil Statutes of Texas, of 1925, exist in the following described territory, to-wit:

The County of Hutchinson in the State of Texas

And I do declare Martial Law in said territory, effective at three o'clock P.M., the twenty-ninth day of September, A.D. 1929, and I hereby direct Brigadier General Jacob F. Wolters to assume supreme command of the situation in the territory affected, subject to the orders of the Governor of Texas, the Commander-in-chief of the miliary forces of this State as given through the Adjutant General.

IN TESTIMONY WHEREOF, I have hereunto signed my name and caused the Seal of the State of Texas to be hereunto affixed at my office at Austin, Texas, this the twenty-eighth day of September, A.D. 1929, at 3:30 o'clock P.M.

(SEAL)

BY THE GOVERNOR   (Signed) Dan Moody,
GOVERNOR OF TEXAS

(Signed) Jane Y. McCallum
Secretary of State.

Reaction to the proclamation and General Orders were applauded by the media generally, by the majority of the towns people, and criticized by those who knew the end of an era of corruption had come.

A few days following Wolters' posting of the proclamation, Governor Moody received a death warning via the Austin police department. The letter, postmarked "Morris Hts. Sta., N.Y., Sept. 30," was addressed to the chief of police:

Mister Chief.
Please be advised that unless your Governor Dan Moody keeps his DAM NOSE out of the doings in Borger one of Austin's undertakers will have a job. HE has more than he can handle when trying to wipe us out.

WE have reached closer & better guarded men
then (*sic*) he EVER will be & REMEMBER?? Chief
— the DEAD carry no tales. This is a personal
WARNING that must NOT be made little of. Our
next move will be ACTION. Our men are closely
watching all Moody's actions. BEWARE
DEATH — DEATH

Texas Rangers took up the investigation of the
threat, and one said that he knew that "a couple of tough
hombres" from Borger were in New York. No one took
the threat of violence to the governor too seriously.

County Judge H. M. Hood received an ace of spades
in the mail. This symbol of death was mailed anony-
mously in Borger on September 26 and was wrapped in a
bit of paper torn from the bottom of an Amarillo paper's
sports page. Hood did not take the warning seriously.

As Provost Marshal, Colonel Louis S. Davidson took
charge of the sheriff's office and jail, the police department, the constable's office, the city jail, the city judge's
office, and all records, books, and papers of the City of
Borger.

He was to disarm all law enforcements officials and
take away their uniforms and badges.

Under General Order No. 3, "the carrying of arms of
any character" was prohibited, and "no firearms, am-
munition, or explosives of any character" were to be
sold, bartered, exchanged, or given away. The soldiers
began searching for weapons immediately, and they,
along with the Texas Rangers, began closing down the illegal stills in and around Borger and confiscating
bootleg whiskey and beer.

Ranger Captain Frank Hamer arrested W. D. Platt,
northwest and across from the Electric City school, and
confiscated three quarts and three pints of wine; one
50-gallon copper still; fifteen empty 50-gallon mash barrels; 600 barrels mash chops. He also arrested Mrs.
George Ward on the Johnson Lease, one mile southwest
of Electric City and recovered seventy-two gallons of

whiskey; one gallon of wine; two 250-gallon copper stills; fifteen 50-gallon mash barrels.

Raids went on twenty-four hours a day. Sometimes the same place of business was hit within hours after the first raid. The guns, games, and alcohol began to accumulate.

Mrs. Betty Ward and J.D. Ward: one Iver Johnson 12 gauge single shot; one Riverside 12 gauge single shot; one double barrel, make and number indistinguishable; one .22 calibre Marlin lever action; one .25-20 Savage, no number; 118 bottles beer.

Blackie Cleveland: one Colt single action revolver; five and a half pints whiskey; sixty-four bottles beer; a half-gallon jug; two bottle cappers.

T.A. Beard and Ed Bailey (back of Betty Jane Hotel): thirty-five bottles beer; 500 empty beer bottles; three 10-gallon crocks.

John Ware: two beer cappers; twenty-four empty bottles broken; three half gallon fruit jars broken.

Jim Hodges, American Boiler and Welding Works: one .38-40 Colt single action revolver; one .30 calibre Remington automatic; one .22 calibre Remington automatic; one 12 gauge Winchester pump.

Sam B. Jones, deputy constable: one .44 calibre S&W Special; one .32 calibre S&W revolver.

Joe Ownbey, sheriff: one .44 S&W Special; one Thompson submachine gun.

C.S. Baird: two .44 S&W Special pistols; one .32 Iver Johnson pistol; one .32 Colt automatic pistol one .30-.30 Winchester rifle; one .25 Winchester rifle.

Borger Athletic Club, C.H. Seaman, manager, and Walter Tydings, owner: one .45 Colt automatic pistol, property of U.S. Army (said to have been left with manager of club by a Reserve officer); one .32 S&W, found in safe.

Two federal agents, George H. Allen and F.W. Harpold of the Treasury Department, had been in Borger for more than a month gathering evidence on bootleggers. Harpold worked undercover.

Thirty-six saloons, blind tigers, gambling halls, and houses of ill repute were raided. Some 115 arrests were made. Another forty-five homes, shops, drugstores were raided, some twice within twenty-four hours. Five members of the liquor ring were taken into custody and charged with violations of the prohibition law. They were Mr. and Mrs. Lewis Crim, Mr. and Mrs. Leroy Dempsey, and Don McCombs. The Crims were old hands at bootlegging, having sold liquor for at least six years, not only in Borger but in other places.

And so it went.

Mayor Glenn A. Pace, who had taken his oath of office on May 9, 1927, resigned under protest on October 14, 1929. He had replaced John R. Miller, who was ousted in 1927 when the Texas Rangers supposedly cleaned the corruption out of Borger the first time. Pace was just as bad, if not worse, than Miller, but the Rangers apparently weren't aware of that when Pace became mayor.

One observer in Borger said the first union he had seen was in Borger and "run by a fellow name of Pace. It was the cooks and waiters. He strong armed it and bagged all the money. He didn't have no connection with no international or nothing, he was just it. He furnished the cooks and the waiters and they paid him $2 a month and that was it. If they didn't pay him that, he had a few boys that took care of 'em, and he was among the first from Borger that run for mayor and was a commissioner."

John P. (Slim) Jones, a well known character and driller, wrote this rather irreverent poem concerning Pace:

You might go straight
A leopard might change his spots

A cat might make a good stepmother to a
  flock of orphan mice
And a hungry wolf might show a nice fat
  lost lamb the way back to the fold,
But it ain't likely.

Resigning during the special session of the city commission, "requested" by Wolters, were Pace, mayor; J.E. Higgins and J.W. Crabtree, commissioners; and W.A. Morton, city secretary. Pace, who had been indicted by a grand jury on October 14, read the following statement:

> I hereby tender my resignation as Mayor of the City of Borger, and member of the Board of City Commissioners, to take effect immediately.

In a statement to the news media, Pace said, "Some man or men of necessity had to be the 'scapegoat' for the wrath of Dan Moody, and it so happened that I, among a few other officals, was chosen for the ordeal, and out of deference and respect for my friends, and the public in general, I resigned, not because I had to, but I felt that the public interest was greater than mine, as martial law, it appears, was declared, not because of failure of the civil powers of this county to function, but because Governor Moody was determined that certain men must resign, hence the drastic action was wrecking the town and inflicting irreparable injury to hundreds of good citizens."

W.A. Henderson replaced Pace as mayor on October 15, 1929. Dyke Cullum and Moe Steinberg were sworn in as commissioners to replace Higgins and Crabtree. Albert N. Mace was named chief of police.

Under an ordinance discharging all employees of the City of Borger in the judicial, administrative, fire, health, and building departments, these, too, were replaced: Almada Wiley, administrative department; Ove E. Overson, judicial department; J.P. Rutherford, health department; J.F. Ford, W.G. Bracken, M.J.

Stockman, D.E. Martin, Lee Hutson, fire department; Joe Clapp, building department; and J.H. Gunnels, street department.

Wolters recalled his feelings concerning the type of men needed to assume administrative and judicial duties in Borger:

"We were concerned about the procurement of real honest-to-God he-men who were clean, capable and honest. We had drafted — and that term is right — Messrs. Henderson and Cullum, both of whom were highly connected by family tradition and in business circles in Texas. We kept open the third place (that of commissioner) until the following day when finally Calhoun (District Attorney Clem Calhoun) decided on Mr. Moe Steinberg, a merchant; and he was elected to fill the third place.

"In the meantime, we were in conference with Judge Hood and the commissioners court with reference to the election of a sheriff and tax collector, for the two offices in Hutchinson County are combined. As sheriff, a bond of $5,000 was required, and as a tax collector, a bond of $175,000. We finally decided on State Ranger C.D. Moore. This gentleman has served six years as sheriff of Falls County, Texas, and made an enviable record. After that he had enlisted in the Ranger force, and as a State Ranger had gained a reputation for probity, intelligence and courage.

"The next problem was the procurement of a Chief of Police. It was not deemed desirable to select any man, no matter how good his record might be, who resided in Borger, Hutchinson County, or anywhere in the Panhandle of Texas. You will recall that when we left Mexia in 1922, the city council had appointed Albert Mace, the former sheriff of Lampasas County, and an ex-Ranger, Chief of Police. Captain Hamer suggested that probably Mr. Mace was 'fed up' of being Chief of Police of so quiet and orderly a city as Mexia had developed into."

Mace accepted, and Wolters said that "for the first time during its hectic career, Borger had a real law-abiding, law-loving Chief of Police." Mace needed five policemen and selected a special agent for an oil company who had never been officially connected with Hutchinson County or Borger and four other men from distant points throughout Texas.

During the first six hours of martial law, ten drunks were arrested. Within three days, not a drunk could be found. Prostitutes, those who remained in town, were picked up, fined $100, and told to leave. Hundreds already had. One staff correspondent for a leading newspaper wrote:

> All of the riff-raff of former days will not be arrested, however. Many are wise enough to keep a step ahead of military rule, and they deserted Borger over the weekend like rats running from a sinking ship. The exodus continued throughout Sunday night. Caravans of cars loaded with household effects and personal belongings are reported to have passed at the south end of Main Street as late as two or three o'clock Monday morning. Cars traveling in the direction of Panhandle were loaded with whatever the deserters could take with them . . .

In the tradition of the Old West, "sundown" orders were given freely; be out of town before sundown or else. Every undesirable the soldiers and Rangers could locate was given one. One of those was a notorious gunman named John Northcutt. Wolters said he was "in Borger pursuing no occupation. He was merely hanging around. He was a bad man to have around. I gave him his choice of a trial for vagrancy before the Provost Judge or a "sun-down order'. He took the latter. Two weeks later he was killed at Wink, another oil field town, by a man whose life it was said he had threatened."

By October 17, 1929, the entrenched criminal ring had been destroyed. Indicted were ex-mayor Glenn A. Pace, Sam Jones, Burlin Milhollon, Cal Baird, Louis Crim, Johnny W. Jones, C.A. Mitchell,

H.O. Taylor, John Ware, and Mrs. Ethel Ware. They were alleged to have organized a liquor line for the purpose of selling and distributing liquor to retail liquor dealers in Hutchinson County and also with arranging "protection for the dealers on condition they dealt only in intoxicating beverages furnished by ring members. Fourteen overt acts were included in the one count of the indictment, issued in blanket form to cover all the defendents. They all pleaded guilty.

However, the murderer of Johnny Holmes still had not been located. A court of inquiry was established to determine who really killed the district attorney and to pinpoint who the criminals in town really were.

7

Who Killed
Johnny Holmes?

There were five prime suspects in the Holmes murder:

Sam Jones, a policeman said to be the crime ring's enforcer.

Former State Representative John Herron White, Borger attorney, who threatened to kill Holmes.

Dr. Louis Dodd, a neighbor of Holmes' and of whom a Texas Ranger said was a "narcotics pusher."

Clint Milhollon and Cal Baird, both law enforcement officers, who had "cussed" Holmes publicly on several occasions.

These names kept cropping up during the military board of inquiry General Wolters established immediately upon arrival in Borger. The board was made up of Colonel O.E. Roberts, Commanding Officer, 143rd Infantry, president; Colonel Louis S. Davidson and Major H.H. Johnson. Asked to sit in were Assistant Attorney General Paul D. Page, Jr., Judge H.M. Hood, District Attorney Clem Calhoun, County Attorney Henry Meyers, and Texas Ranger Captains Frank Hamer and Tom Hickman.

Under Special Order No. 3, more than eighty witnesses were called to testify. Among them were A.C. Embry, Juanita McClure, Mittie Bell Peterson, Jim Crane, Hoyt Embry, George Custer, Tex Thrower, J.W. Crabtree, J.M. Higgins, George Tarrant, Gus Barrington, Mrs. Clint Milhollon, Verlin Milhollon, Sheriff Joe Ownbey, Mayor Glenn Pace, Mr. and Mrs. J.A. McClaren, C.A. Mitchell, Cal Baird, Helen McClure, Phil Trock, Attorney John Herron White, C.A. Mitchell, J.T. Alvis, Jim Hodges, Mrs. C.R. Stahl, Henry J. Letterman, C.R. Stahl, Dexter Kirkpatrick, Mrs. Sam Jones, R.R. Cook, Dr. S.A. Southall, Helen Hindman, J.V. Grubbs, Helen Valliant, Mrs. Lillian Holcomb, Johnnie Ford, Mrs. John A. Holmes, Max Whitman, Bill Casaway, Bill Bates, John Farmer, Mr. and Mrs. Wayne O'Keefe, and John Ware.

Others were called in for questioning as the investigations progressed.

The first session lasted fourteen hours, and while some interesting facts developed, the board concluded that never had so many said so little. Wolters observed later that "it soon became evident that persons, good, bad, or indifferent were afraid to talk. I began to realize what the trouble was. The sheriff, the mayor, and the suspended commissioner of police were not appearing in public. In fact, after testifying before the board of inquiry during its first and second sessions, they were out of the county; but the principal law violators, well known characters in town, were still walking the streets."

Testimony before the board wasn't for public consumption, but secret or not, everyone knew who was to testify, and few of the witnesses, if any, were going to tell everything they knew.

Sheriff Ownbey did trace the movement of Holmes' slayer by working backwards from the car in which the killer escaped, the board learned.

The car had been parked two blocks away from Holmes' house, and Ownbey and his deputies traced the footsteps of a man walking fast and deliberately. They

111

led to the rear of a vacant house next door south of Holmes' residence, and then to a small niche formed by a jutting back porch. The killer was hidden from view from the street by the house and shrubbery, which ran along the entire north wall next to the attorney's house and driveway.

The ground had been trampled considerably and leaves had been plucked from the shrubbery and torn into tiny bits by the nervous killer. Holmes had driven his car into the garage and the assassin shot him as he was reaching up to close the door. Holmes' mother-in-law, Mrs. Donna Greene, heard the shots and looked out of the rear window of the house. She saw Holmes collapse and saw the killer stoop over the body, either to see that Holmes was dead or to check through his coat pockets. Then, the killer ran across the neighboring backyard, jumped a three-foot high fence and ran north down the alley past a one-story stucco apartment house. Although he didn't step forward at the time of the initial investigation, there was a witness. A man had opened his apartment door and had seen the running man, although he didn't see his face. He said later he felt there was something familiar about the man's body shape and the way he was running.

The killer kept on going until he was two blocks away, where he shucked the five empty shells and an unfired cartridge from his gun. The deputies found them. They were from a .38 calibre special and had been greased as a precaution against jamming.

The assassin drove away in a light colored sedan. Witnesses said he was about six feet tall, between 160 and 180 pounds, wore a large white hat and a dark sweater or lumberjacket.

Some people felt the sheriff department's investigation was rather perfunctory, among them Mrs. Holmes, who was quite bitter over her husband's death. She told Rangers and the court about the prediction of friends and threats by his enemies that "he wouldn't live to serve out his term of office." She spoke of the battle he had been waging against lawlessness in Borger. "There wasn't more than one man to help him. The rest of them were afraid. When there is no one to help, you have to play a lone hand. He never had any fear. He was all I had and now they've taken him."

Several months before his death, Holmes expressed similar feelings in a letter to Governor Moody:

> It is discouraging to a district attorney to have to fight alone and see the criminal element defy the law and run over the rights of people. I can clean up conditions here in this county if you will only help me. The people of this district relieved you of your fight with Curtis Douglas as district attorney by putting him out of office, and now they expect you to help them by giving their district attorney some assistance.

Moody sent a Ranger to assist Holmes shortly after receipt of the DA's letter.

Mrs. Holmes wanted her husband to resign and move to Amarillo. Holmes, however, was confident that the respect for the district attorney's office would protect him, and took the threats against him lightly. He was urged to carry a pistol, but refused. He clung to the idea that he would not be harmed. Allen S. Johnson, a local constable, said he had visited Holmes that afternoon before his death and found him "cheeful and confident. He even disclosed his plans to run for the office of district judge, which was recently vacated by the resignation of Judge Newton P. Willis."

The Rangers felt they had a motive for the killing and had an affidavit concerning an alleged plot between city and county officials. The county officials deplored the statement, of course, and J.W. Crabtree, chief of police, offered to bet $1,000 that when the "right party is

arrested, the city and county officers will arrest him."
Few believed him.

One of those questioned by the Court was R. A. Murray, who came to Borger on March 26, 1926, to operate a confectionary stand. He lived at 820 N. Main.

Q. Have you any ideas valuable to this Court as to the killing of Johnny Holmes?

A. No sir, I do not have.

Q. Have you heard any talk about it?

A. Just general talk around town.

Q. Have you tried to find out?

A. Well, only just listening to people talk and discussing their opinion.

Q. Have you formed any opinion from what you have heard?

A. I could hardly say.

Q. You have an idea in your head haven't you?

A. It always looked to me like it was a paid job from the general surroundings.

Q. This is a secret court, Murray, and what you state here will not be divulged. What have you got in the way of a lead or clue or information that can be put to use by this court in this investigation?

A. The night he was killed I heard a whistle blow three times. You know where the filling station is by my place, and I was standing there talking. It blew three times, as you remember, about three or four seconds apart, and they said that was a fire, and I said, 'No, that must be calling in the law,' and someone else said, 'Let's go down the street to see whether it is a fire,' and got in my car and when I got to the city hall, there was a bunch gathered there, and we drove around the block, and a man who runs the tailor business this side of Hoyt's Drug Store, next to the barber shop, and I asked him what the trouble was, and he said that Johnny Holmes was shot, and I asked him where Johnny Holmes lived and he told me he lived in the stucco house over next to

114

X MARKS THE scene of Holmes' assassination. The assassin lurked in the bushes at the side of the house. He fired five shots at Holmes, three hitting him.

THE KILLER RAN through this yard next to the Holmes home to the alley, heading north.

the Ferndale Apartments, and I drove over there, and the undertaker had done got him.

I went on back home, and Lee Huddleston came up there and called me off and said, 'I am going to have to arrest you and take you down to the station,' and I said, 'What is all this about?' He said, 'Holmes has been killed.' I said, 'I'll tell you something. I will go down as a citizen, but not under arrest in a case like that, and that any way I could be of assistance I would gladly do so,' and he said, 'All right, come on down,' and in twenty or thirty minutes I went down, and there was quite a crowd there by then.

Q. Were there any officers there when you got there?

A. Well, let's see. Johnny Ford and Sam Jones and the mayor were running around there talking to one another, and I think J.B. Lee and Creek, some four or five of them was hauling them down in cars.

Q. What is the undercurrent among the people around town as to how that thing happened?

A. I have heard people express different opinions. I heard some of them say he was killed by one man alone ... most of them said it was a paid job, and they claimed the man stopped over him after he had shot him, and if he was paid to do it, he was paid to be sure he was dead.

Another to testify was S.E. Wilson, who had lived in Borger from the very start.

Q. Mr. Wilson, where were you on the night of the 13th when Johnny Holmes was killed?

A. Well, I guess I was sitting in front — I don't know what street that is. I was sitting on the street by the city hall that faces by the Anderson Drug Store on a box.

Q. You know Mr. Holmes, did you not?

A. Yes, sir, very well.

Wilson said he was doing some window shopping with a man named Blackie, stopping to look at a sale of women's coats and things in the K.C. Store. "We looked in the next window and they had some men's stuff in that marked $6.98 and $25.50, I believe that was the

HOLMES' MOTHER-IN-LAW and wife came running out the door on the left to find the district attorney dying on the driveway leading to the garage.

JOHNNY HOLMES LIVED here while a district attorney in Borger. He was shot down in this driveway.

THE KILLER OF Johnny Holmes ran past these apartments in Borger. The apartments, still standing, are just south of Holmes' home.

price, and we turned around and Mr. Holmes was standing on the sidewalk looking across the street. He said, 'Hidy, fellows,' and I said, 'Hidy-do, Mr. Holmes.'

Q. Now, about what time was that?

A. Well, I couldn't tell the exact time. It was between nine, between, I judge, nine thirty and ten o'clock . . . We walked over to the window where the suits were on display and were standing there talking, and I heard him say, 'Honey, here's the one,' and I just turned and looked back and I seen two ladies coming out of the Greene Shop. I knew his wife. I met his wife up there. I had been to his office several times and I had met his wife up at the office. I don't know whether I knew his mother-in-law; I have never been in that place. There were two cars parked there and they got in the car and backed the car out and we still stood there and there were other cars . . . He got in the car and drove down and met her and they went to the pressing shop and what he said I don't know, only I heard him say he wanted him to come and get a suit of clothes. I heard him say that, that he had a little suit of clothes on the back gallery to be sure and get it because he was going to Amarillo or . . . no, he had to go to Canadian to court. I believe it was Canadian or some town to court, but he was going to Amarillo."

Wilson and Blackie moved on, talking, sitting down on a box near one of the corners. Wilson told the Court he heard the first whistle. "It didn't go very loud. I said, 'Well, there is a fire, Blackie,' and he says 'No,' then about that time it gave another one and Blackie said, 'No, that is a police signal. I have been living in this hotel over two years and I have heard that so much I know it.' The third time they blew it we got up and walked over there. In the meantime, we met two policemen. I seen John Ware and Cunningham and a man by the name of John Northcutt all coming across the street over there when they first blew the whistle. I walked over to the city hall, and, of course, there was seventy-five or a hundred people gathered over at the city hall, and the first thing I seen, I seen Johnny Ford and J.D. Lee come down toward the Marland Hotel and pull in."

Further questioning brought out that Wilson had heard that Ford and Lee had been at the "Jim Joe, where they have these wrestling matches."

Deputy Sheriff Jim Crane, former sheriff at Childress, 1919-1924, had been working on the Holmes murder. Asked by the court if he had any information to give, Crane answered, "I think that I have, Mr. Calhoun. I could not say that I have any at all, though, except mere conversation."

Q. Where were you the night of the killing?

A. At the boxing match at the Colisseum. Cal (Baird) and I were sitting together.

Q. What city officers did you see there that night?

A. I saw Clint Milhollon, Johnny Ford, and I didn't see Sam Jones at all until just before the fight was over. I saw him come in.

Q. Was that before or after the killing?

A. It must have been about the time of the killing or perhaps just after. I don't know just what time it happened. I didn't see Crabtree. I didn't see Pace.

Q. Did you see M.K. Brown.

A. I didn't see him.

Q. Did you see Sam Jones leave the fight?

A. No, I didn't, Judge. He came in just before the fight was over.

Q. When was the fight over with reference to the sounding of the siren?

A. I didn't hear that. It must have been after the call that he came in.

Q. Did you leave the fight to go to the scene of the killing?

A. I didn't know about the killing until the fight was over. But I think he came in sometime after the killing was over. I figure he did.

119

Q. How was he dressed when he came into the fight?

A. I believe he had on a light pair of trousers, kind of gray, and a vest to match. I don't think he had a coat on. He had on a soft shirt, something like Mr. Hamer's over there, as well as I remember. He had on a hat — quite light — it was a soft hat, smaller than mine.

Q. When did you hear about the killing?

A. When the fight was over. John Harris, a Phillips Petroleum Co. superintendent, told me Holmes had been shot. Then Glenn Pace told me.

Crane said he had gotten his car and "whirled at the first turn going west to Johnny's house between the Betty Jane Hotel and the Panhandle Power & Light Company." He arrived at the scene about forty-five minutes after the shooting.

Q. Was there anything unusual in the appearance of Sam Jones that night after he came to the scene of the murder?

A. No, not that I know.

Q. Anything unusual in the appearance of Pace?

A. No. Of course, I heard some things that kind of put me to thinking. I heard Brownie was at Sam's house asking for him that night.

Q. What kind of gun does Sam Jones carry?

A. Sam Jones did for a long time carry a Smith & Wesson.

Q. Didn't he carry the same gun any length of time?

A. He didn't carry the same pistol very long. He carried a .44 Smith & Wesson for a long time, but he went broke and I think sold it.

Q. Did you ever see him carry a .38?

A. I could not say positively. I think he had a .38 S&W.

The court learned a fact here, a rumor there, and various names kept cropping up on who might have wanted to kill Holmes. Holmes, the court learned, was not too popular among city officials and law enforcement officers because of his persistence. Charlie Smith's testimony brought that out quite clearly.

Smith, who was living in Gruver at the time the court convened, had been a deputy sheriff under Joe Ownbey and had worked for Holmes, too. Shortly following Holmes' death, Smith received a threatening letter telling him not to investigate the murder.

Q. What did the letter say?

A. It just said that they understood I was going to stay here for this next term of court. If I did, I would never live to see the term of court over with. That was all it said, so I got it and read it. It kinda puzzled me for a little bit. I know there had been threats made against me the other way, so I just tore it up to keep my wife from seeing it."

Judge Hood wanted Smith to name "three men in Borger that did this killing."

A. I said three men that I could pick and I believe I would have the man.

He named Sam Jones, Clint Milhollon, and Cal Baird, and added, "and I'm not taking anything back. I have talked to Johnny a whole lot, and Sam Jones was the only man in the county that he was really afraid of, that I could ever get him to say anything about, and knowing Clint Milhollon like I do and things that Cal Baird said about me and other officers in the county, that just made me believe it was one of the three of them that has done it.

Q. Did you ever hear the mayor or any city police forces say anything about Johnny Holmes?

A. No, sir, not to me.

Q. Have you heard of their saying that to anybody?

A. No, sir, I never heard of that in my life. Of course, if a fellow had said that — I have told Johnny many times he had better be careful or they would kill him.

Q. What did he think about it?

A. He didn't seem to think much about it. He would just tell me, 'you be careful you wouldn't be killed.' He told me that in Spearman.

Q. Did Johnny Holmes go armed, did he carry a pistol?

A. Well, now, I don't think he did. I gave him a little old pistol myself, one of those double barrel (derringers) and he started to carry it and told me he just couldn't get that if he was to need it.

Q. What?

A. He couldn't get hold of it if he was to need it, and a fellow over at Panhandle gave him a .32 automatic — the sheriff, I believe it was. He told him, he says, 'Johnny, carry that all the time,' and I went out with him a time or two out in the canyons here to shoot it and he would shoot with it, and finally he just told me, he says, 'Charlie, I couldn't do no good with a gun.'

The court kept picking up the street talk that Holmes was fixing to get himself killed if he didn't lay off his investigation into the liquor, drug, and prostitution traffic in town. His friends told him the story was going around that he'd "never live out his term of office," so Holmes was aware of the furor he was creating among the lawless, and he didn't care. Charlie Hale, one of the court's witnesses, said "I talked to Johnny and he talked to me about the rumors he was liable to be killed. He said that he got these guys all handled up and he said some of them was liable to try to kill him or do something to him."

John T. Buckle, another witness, said pretty much the same thing. "We were discussing the prosecution by him (Holmes) of Pace and Sam Jones and that bunch, and I told him if I was him that I would be careful for my physical safety as he and I discussed those things over, having been partners for quite awhile, and he told, he said, 'I am going to stay on until they get out of office or break up this ring.' And he said, 'They are not coming to my face, and if they ever do anything to me, it will have to be from the dark,' and I told him that that was the way it might happen, and that he ought to be guarded against it."

Tom Hughes, brought before the investigators, accused Johnny Ford and Clint Milhollon of Holmes' murder.

"The information that I will give you is an idea of mine that might give you a clue to the assassination," he said. "I want to show you where it is an idea of mine, and you can draw your idea."

Hughes said that Ford had come to Borger because he was "sent for," and when he arrived he went to work for the city at $200 a month. "None of us drawed over $150, but they put him on at $200. It looked strange they would import a pimp and a whoremonger and give him $200 a month and the rest of us only getting $150 a month. I don't know what Milhollon drew, whether $200 or not, but I will say this that Milhollon was just as fat and sassy as I am, and that within three days after the assassination of the district attorney, I noticed him going down, and he told me the other day that he had fallen off fifty pounds, and that the doctors couldn't tell what was the matter with him, and I don't think there is nothing the matter with him only he is just grieving himself to death over something."

Q. He was not sick prior to the killing?

A. Not a day in his life, I don't reckon; just as fat as could be.

Q. Did you see him the day immediately preceding the killing?

A. I guess I hadn't seen him maybe for two or three days before then when I seen him pass down there. I haven't been around the station any, you might say, since the 15th of July. Another thing I will tell you. I can't tell you nothing positively as it will have to come through another fellow, but the night Johnny Holmes was assassinated, a fellow living right across the street (I don't know who he was as they didn't tell me his name) but told me conscientiously about this fellow running from Johnny Holmes' house.

Q. West from Holmes' street?

A. I don't know which way it was, but he said across the street. I don't even know where Holmes lived myself, but he said this fellow was a tall slender fellow with a white hat on, and that fills Ford's description pretty well. Here is my idea about it. Milhollon sat in the car and Johnny Ford did the work. That is a supposition of my own since the way things have panned out since then. Milhollon is falling off and grieving himself to death about something.

Hughes, a close friend of Texas Ranger J.B. Wheatley, suggested the Court ask Ed Albin, owner of C&A Tailor Shop, about what the neighbor had seen.

"Ed and Johnny were warm friends, but Ed is afraid if he gets mixed up in it he will get assassinated, too. I am not afraid of all of them in the day time, but in darkness, they will slip up and do anybody like they did Johnny Holmes. I don't think they imported a man here at all because that city bunch never was far away from home, and you know they would have to go through too many strangers to get a murderer down here. It is bound to have been somebody in town. It looks very plain that somebody right here in town did it, and I believe Clint Milhollon and Johnny Ford, if they were put in a place and kept awake for sixty hours would tell everything. Have a man sit right there with them and take their shift, and keep them awake. That is the worst punishment in the world."

John Herron White, attorney and former state legislator, was another suspect in the Holmes killing.

He and Holmes never got along, and the street talk was that White had said that he would kill Holmes if he ever met him on the sidewalks of Borger.

The court asked White if he had made any statements about Holmes following his death.

A. No, sir. I might have been talking. I don't remember what I said, but I might have made statements to the effect about the dirty way it was to get a man by shooting him from the back . . . something like that.

Q. Think before you answer this question. Did you ever make a statement on the street to the effect that if you had met John Holmes in the street you would have killed him?

A. Right after he had me arrested ...

Q. (Interrupting) I mean after his death.

A. No.

Q. You sure of that.

A. I heard the same thing, and a friend of mine told me the other day that he had heard that I had said if this fellow hadn't killed him, I would have.

Q. You are sure you made no such statement?

A. No, I never made any such statement.

White told the court that he was home with his wife the night Holmes was killed, but that he had left his office about 9 p.m. and had seen Holmes and Holmes' wife "at the Orange Stand." White and his wife were in their car and Mrs. Holmes saw them and said something to her husband. White turned to his wife and said, "There is a dirty rat."

Q. You and Johnny Holmes had had a controversy a short time before he was killed.

A. Yes, sir.

When White was a state representative, Holmes requested the legislature to approve a bill authorizing the hiring of special investigators to assist him in Borger. White objected to the bill because, he told the Court, "an objection had come from so many business houses at Borger, and so many people, that I didn't think it would be advisable at this time."

Holmes requested to speak to the Senate State Affairs Committee on the matter and was questioned thoroughly by its members.

How many murders have been committed in Hutchinson County since the oil boom?

Holmes: "Twenty-two or twenty-three."

Has the sheriff ever failed to put these murderers in jail?

Holmes: "No."

Who was the district attorney when the slot machines and gambling holes were wide open in Borger? Holmes. "I was."

Has the sheriff ever failed to cooperate with you in any instance?

Holmes: "No."

Then Senator Archie Parr asked, "What in the name of God do you want special investigators up there for?" Parr then pointed out that a similiar bill passed in another county some years ago, and it had led to two or three killings within a short time.

White then told the court that "until that time Holmes' attitude toward me, I thought, was all right. He claimed that I double crossed him in it, and this and that, that I didn't treat him fair on his bill."

Within a short time following the defeat of the special investigators bill, Holmes issued a warrant for White's arrest, charging him with "forging a name to a divorce waiver." White made $1,000 bond and returned to Austin. "When I got to Austin the front pages of the newspapers had LEGISLATOR FACES CHARGE AS A FELON, CHARGED WITH FORGERY. JOHN HERRON WHITE FACES CHARGES, etc. Gentlemen, when you see something you didn't do, or hadn't done, it will make you mad, and if I had seen Mr. Holmes at the time, I would have settled it with him right then and there. I came back to Borger and asked in a roundabout way how it got in the newspaper, and the newspaper said that Mr. Holmes personally came down and put it into the papers. From that time on I couldn't be considered a friend of Holmes."

General Wolters then asked White again, "You didn't kill Holmes?"

White: "No, sir."

Wolters: "Are you sure you didn't?

White: "I am sure I didn't."

Wolters: "I don't think so, either. I never did."

E. L. Butts, a bookkeeper for the Whitlock and Smith Salvage Company, told the military court that he had some information to pass on about the Holmes murder.

Q. Mr. Butts, have you received intimidating or threatening letters within the past few days?

A. Yes, sir, yesterday I received it.

Q. The envelope is dated October 10th, dated at Gewhit with an ace of spades and note addressed to yourself. Have you any idea who sent that? Have you been spreading any information or talking about the city here in Borger?

A. Well, I have just talked more or less, but not publicly expressed my opinion.

Q. Now, the information you have in connection with the Holmes case. What was that?

A. That is, of course, hearsay. I heard that Sis at Pantex said that there was — they would never catch the murderer of Johnny Holmes.

Q. Did you hear her make the remark?

A. No, I didn't hear her, but it was told directly by a fellow that did hear her.

Q. Who was it?

A. Whitlock, J. H. Whitlock, and he told me and asked me to tell Judge Hood. It was a threat against Judge Hood this way that I heard it. He didn't want me to tell where I got the information, but I had to tell it, because I couldn't very well keep that . . . She said they would never catch the murderer and that it was done by four men, a conspiracy between four men, and one — and three of them was bootleggers and one was a man that had been collecting. She didn't say whether they were officers or just collecting for protection, and that they did the job and that they were going to kill Judge Hood; they had plotted on killing him, too, and I told Judge Hood that and I haven't told anyone else, only Judge Meyers.

Q. What do you suppose caused you to receive the letter?

A. I don't have any idea. I will tell you the truth. I thought it was just a joke somebody was playing on me more than anything else.

Butts told the court that Pantex Sis probably would deny the whole story, and he repeatedly asked the court not to mention his name if they brought her in for questioning.

Q. Why don't you want your name mentioned.

A. Well, I just don't want to be in any danger down there. I don't care anything about her. I just rather my name would be out.

Q. Just like a whole lot of these people, you don't want to be shot at in the dark. I am trying to get your idea, whether you think there is actual danger as to persons testifying if they have information before this court.

A. I believe there is.

Q. Where do you think that danger would likely come from, from whom, who would harm you? Do you feel danger exists through the officers?

A. No, I never did fear the officers very much. I think whoever it is is connected with the ring here. The people that killed Johnny Holmes I think would do most anything.

Another suspect the court took an interest in was Dr. Louis Dodd, who lived two houses down from Johnny Holmes.

Although there is little documentation to pinpoint the stories concerning Dodd, there is some evidence that he might have been dealing in drugs. He was known to the Texas Rangers as a "narcotics pusher."

Holmes apparently was aware of Dr. Dodd's activities as there was some indication he was going to file charges against Dodd in Federal Court in Amarillo on September 14, the day following Holmes' murder. Dodd could not be found the day following the shooting!

A telephone operator, questioned by the court, testified that she had heard a phone conversation between a lady from Pampa and someone else "three to four days after Holmes was killed. They told us he wasn't there; he was on his way to New York." The suggestion was that Dodd was headed east.

However, one story circulated several years after the shooting was that Dodd really went to California and was killed during a shoot-out with the highway patrol. He is said to have been selling drugs and was caught, choosing to shoot it out. He lost. The rest of the story is that the gun he had was a similar calibre to the one that killed Holmes.

Nothing very solid was brought out about Dodd during the inquiry, though. Not enough, anyway, to place him very high on the suspect list.

There was a witness to the shooting, however. He was Hoyt Embry, who had been visiting his older brother, A.C. Embry, who lived in an apartment approximately one block north of Holmes' house. Hoyt heard the shots and the screams of Holmes' wife and mother-in-law. He went to the door of the apartment and saw a man "coming down to the end" of the alley. "I would say he would weigh from 175 up . . . a short, heavyset fellow. He wasn't so tall. He was running heavy and bending when he passed our place there."

Hoyt added that the man had on a khaki outfit and either a coat or a lumber jacket, "because I could see the shirt where it was open." The man wore a small hat, light colored. He was from twelve to fifteen feet from Hoyt when he ran by.

Q. Who was it?

A. I don't know.

Q. Haven't you told someone about being downtown and seeing that fellow and telling your brother that that was the man you saw?

A. It wasn't just like that. I told him it 'resembled' the fellow.

Q. You know who it is.

A. I couldn't be positive.

Q. I don't want you to lie, but don't you hold back here if you know who that man is.

A. I wouldn't for a minute. If I knew who he was I would go out of my way toward bringing him to justice. That is exactly the way I feel about that.

Q. Well, your brother told you who that was.

A. Yes, sir. Sam Jones. He was about that size fellow, but really I couldn't say. I couldn't get a clear view of him, to tell the truth, when I saw him running. I looked to see if there wasn't someone behind him. When I heard the shots there at the garage and he came by, I looked back up the alley to see if there was anything after him.

Q. Did you receive any warning before you left (town); anybody threaten you?

A. No.

The questioning of Hoyt continued for a long time, probably because the court felt it was nearing something solid concerning Holmes' killer, although Hoyt kept backing away from naming Sam Jones definitely as the man he saw.

Q. Did you write down and show your brother or anybody else the name of the man you thought did the killing at any time?

A. No.

Q. Up at the office, which one of you was it talked to the engineer at the El Reno Ice Company, and when asked who it was, which one of you wrote it out on a piece of paper — the name 'Sam Jones?'

A. I don't recall doing that at all. I never mentioned his name to anyone except you fellows.

Hoyt was asked if anyone had intimidated him or his brother, suggesting that "it would be best for them not to know too much about this thing." Hoyt denied that anyone had. However, further questioning brought out that Hoyt just might have changed his mind about the person he saw.

Q. Now, when did you first decide that you were not so certain about it being Sam Jones.

A. Sunday night.

Q. Then from the 18th of September until the 29th of September inclusive, you had the opinion that it was Sam Jones.

A. Yes, sir.

Q. When was it then you first became uncertain?

A. I was laying there in bed and just got to studying. I was thinking, just figuring, that if they were going to do anything like that they would get a man to come in here to do it. I just got to studying that probably he didn't do it.

Q. Is that what caused you to change your mind, that you thought probably they would have somebody else do it?

A. No, I got to thinking he didn't look like him in the face. Then I got to comparing and studying over and comparing and I thought if they did anything like that that is what they would do.

Q. You have no fear of going on the witness stand and getting what Holmes did if you told it.

A. Yes, I do for this reason. I don't have no fear in a way unless they get hold of it. I know if they put him out they would me too. I don't think they will get hold of it. I think when I am talking, I am talking absolutely secretly.

Q. Well, don't you know that you might be called on to testify in court in a trial of Sam Jones.

A. Certainly.

Q. Well, you knew that all the time.

A. Yes, I thought they would call me.

Q. Isn't it a fact that that is just what you don't want to do.

A. I don't care for it.

Q. Did your brother say anything to you about anybody telling him that 'it would just take one more shot to put him out' if he didn't keep out of this and keep his mouth shut?

A. He didn't tell me in those words, but said 'just a matter of another shot.'

Hoyt said that "a little fellow" was standing near him and a couple of women who were part of the crowd which gathered near Holmes' house after the shooting. They were talking and suddenly the little man made the remark that "it was just a matter of one more shot." Hoyt said the "lady made the remark that somebody ought to tell the law, that he looks suspicious."

The man left, and nothing further was heard about him. Following more questions along the lines of description, clothing, and impressions, Hoyt was excused as a witness.

Evidence, however slight, seemed to be building up against Sam Jones. His name kept cropping up in the testimony of witnesses. Tex Thrower, a driver for the El Reno Ice Company, said he thought he saw Jones walk up the alley where the killing took place. "He was a rather large fellow, heavy man about Sam Jones' build. I didn't see his face, but seeing him walk down the street looked like the way he walked and looked like Sam Jones. All I thought of then, when I seen him, I said to myself, 'That's one of our Borger officers . . . some law.'"

Thrower added that the man wore a medium sized white hat, a solid colored jacket, and was with another man in a Buick Six sedan, a lighter green than the one used by city police. Further questioning finally got a solid answer from Thrower. "It was Sam Jones."

Q. Of course, you know these proceedings are secret, and we are not going to go out and tell what you tell us here. Everytime since then, you have thought, 'that's the man who killed Holmes,' haven't you?

A. Yes, I have thought about it.

★ ★ ★

Of the five suspects, Sam Jones appeared to be the most likely candidate, yet there was nothing concrete in

132

the testimony of the witnesses that said, "Sam Jones did it." The court did have a strong "maybe," however, and passed on its information to the Texas Rangers for consideration and action, if any.

The more than eighty witnesses gave the military and Rangers information about kangaroo courts, bootlegging, prostitution, payoffs, car thefts, locations of stills, questionable practices concerning kickbacks on contracts awarded by the city, naming names, places, and dates.

Those who hadn't already left town were jailed or warrants were filed for their apprehension. The town began to take on some semblance of other law-abiding towns in the Panhandle.

8

The Arrest

The entrenched criminal ring was finished. Honest, capable officers replaced Ownbey and Crabtree, and new city officials settled down to putting the town on a stable, more normal footing.

Martial law, which began September 28, 1929, ended officially at 4 p.m., October 29. General Wolters' troops, however, withdrew from Borger at 3:50 p.m., October 18, following the closing of the Provost Marshal's office at 12 noon, October 17, under Special Order No. 259. The detachment arrived in Fort Worth at 8:30 a.m., October 19, and the officers and enlisted men were sent to their respective homes.

During the nineteen days of martial law, 87 search warrants were issued to the Texas Rangers; 50 houses were searched and the occupants questioned; 78 summons were issued; 49 cases were tried in the Provost Court; 17 persons were filed on in the State Court; 9 persons were filed on in Federal Court; 356 meals were served to prisoners held in the city jail; $1,058 in fines was assessed; $100 was remitted by the Court; $931 in total fines collected; 37 days worked out on fines by prisoners; $90 was due on fines from prisoners; 239 permits to purchase 509 boxes of shells were issued; 307 permits to carry shotguns for hunting purposes only were issued.

The nineteen days the military detachment was

operative cost the state's taxpayers $15,084.43, which included $6,421.95 payroll; $1,567.03 subsistence; $3,546.71 transportation, and $3,548.74 miscellaneous.

Johnny Holmes' assassin was not apprehended during martial law; however, the Texas Rangers were not idle. Using information they received during and following the court of inquiry, they finally arrested former deputy constable Sam Jones and Jim Hodges, manager of the American Boiler Works, on November 2, 1929, for Holmes' murder. It is probable that Hodges was the driver of the getaway car.

Deputy Sheriff Red Burton filed the charges against the two men. He went to Hobbs, New Mexico, to pick up Jones, who had been indicted for a liquor law violation. Hodges, arrested at his Borger home, had once been prosecuted by Holmes and freed in a pipe theft case. He also maintained his innocence of Holmes' shooting during intensive questioning by the sheriff's department.

Just what evidence the department collected against Jones and Hodges apparently has been lost, but news accounts indicate that it was solid enough to take before a grand jury. Both were indicted on November 16 with Jones specifically charged with "voluntarily and with malice aforethought of killing J. A. Holmes by shooting him with a gun."

Clem Calhoun, district attorney, said in a news story that "more evidence against Jones and Hodges has been collected since their arrest," and that "neither man had made any statement and that the indictments rested on the testimony of others."

Both Jones and Hodges were spirited out of Borger on November 17 and taken to Fort Worth. Late that same afternoon, they were removed from the Fort Worth jail for "an unannounced destination."

Calhoun told reporters that "they were removed for safe keeping." Just what that meant isn't clear because there apparently were no indications of a jail break or "other violence."

135

Attorneys for Jones and Hodges were seeking their release on bond, but they had to get them to Stinnett for a habeas corpus hearing. A news story said that "attorneys who have played hide and seek with Hutchinson County officers for better part of a week in an effort to obtain bonds for Sam Jones and Jim Hodges finally caught up with their quarry in Wichita Falls, November 21, and obtained service on the deputy in charge of the prisoners.

"Deputy Sheriff Mack (Red) Burton was served with the summons about an hour after he had placed Jones and Hodges in the county jail in Wichita Falls. Burton and Sheriff W. G. Braley of Wichita County were ordered by Judge P. A. Martin to produce the prisoners for a habeas corpus hearing at 9 o'clock, Friday, November 22.

"The petition for the writ charged Burton had removed the prisoners from Hutchinson County illegally and deprived them unlawfully of their liberty." The action was the third of its kind in a week. Similar attempts had been made at Stinnett and Fort Worth. In each of those two cases it was impossible to obtain service as Burton had fled with the prisoners "in the nick of time."

Bond of $9,000 each was set for Jones and Hodges on November 23, but both were still jailed in Stinnett. The habeas corpus hearing was marked by a verbal and near physical encounter between the district attorney and the attorneys for the two men. The DA, Clem Calhoun, said he did not intend "to show his hand" by revealing the evidence against the two. That remark was interpreted by W. C. Wicher, attorney for Jones, as an insult and the clash between the two was avoided when a deputy sheriff threatened Calhoun with a "bust on the nose."

Jones, one to take advantage of his opportunities, whined about his alleged mistreatment during the hide-and-seek tactics of Calhoun and Red Burton. "I'm tired of staying in jail," he said, asserting that he was innocent of the charges. "This matter of being taken around county jails, handcuffed, is embarrasing to me. I wish newspapers would forget me."

On November 26, Hodges was released on bonds totaling $9,000. In addition to the murder bond of $7,500, he was required to furnish $1,500 on a liquor indictment. His bondsmen were W.S. Christian and Martin Keith. It wasn't until November 29 that Jones was able to make bond on $7,500, but he was not released because he did not make the $1,500 on a second indictment for a liquor law violation. K.R. McNutt, a landowner, provided his bond.

Then, on December 1, 1929, the newspaper headlines read:

9 Men, 5 Former Borger Officials Face U.S. Charge

And the newspaper story said that "life is a matter of making just one bond after another to Sam Jones, deposed Borger deputy constable.

"Today he made $1,500 bond on an indictment for a liquor violation. The day before he made $7,500 bond in connection with the slaying of D.A. John A. Holmes.

"And today, just as he had packed his belongings and was getting ready to leave the Hutchinson County jail, he was informed that federal charges of conspiracy to violate the National Prohibition Act had been filed against him. Another bond had to be made."

Also charged were former Mayor Glenn A. Pace, Chief Deputy Jim Crane; former deputy Cal Baird, former constable C.A. Mitchell, former Deputy Constable Jack Payne, H.O. Taylor, E.L. Lantron, Louis Weitzman, and Louis Crim. Bonds were set at $5,000 and $10,000. All were taken to the Potter County jail in Amarillo. Officials said it was one of the "most expensive group of prisoners ever to take a bus ride," estimating that bonds would total between $60,000 and $120,000.

On December 3, former Sheriff Joe Ownbey, Burlin

Millhollon (also spelled Berlin Milhollon), E.T. Blassingame, R.T. Macey, and John Harkness (who was in the penitentiary at the time) were charged with being members of a bootlegging ring. The charges were made following an extensive investigation by federal prohibition officers over a period of several months.

Jones finally got out of jail on $10,000 bond.

Former Mayor Glenn Pace was cleared of all charges pending against him in Hutchinson County on December 21, 1929.

Judge Pickens said that the "indictment herein was returned through error and mistake in that the defendent (Pace) in consideration of his resignation as mayor of Borger was granted immunity in the indictment and for this case it should be dismissed by virtue of an agreement." Pace remained under federal indictment, however.

Then, on December 29, a Wewoka, Oklahoma, man confessed to killing Holmes. Borger officers, however, talked with the man, Henry York, and came away convinced he was "fabricating when he said he participated in the killing." York was being held in Seminole County jail on a charge of robbery with firearms.

Statements made by York were checked with the facts of the case, and officers determined that he could not have been involved.

Apparently there were some who were not satisfied with the results of the murder investigation, because on May 23, 1930, Borger Chief of Police Mace wrote to General Wolters that he had "some very important information in the Holmes case."

A Major C.H. Machen was investigating on his own time and using his own money to "cinch the evidence we already have," the chief told Wolters. "Now it is going to be very important that a certain man is gotten out of N.M. back into Texas, and Maj. is lined up to where I am sure that this can be carried out if we will help him bear this expence [sic] and as you know there is a fund ap-

propriated for the apprenhension of Criminals in the hands of the Gov. If not there this expence [*sic*] could be arranged to come for the Adj. Gen. office, or a part of the Ranger appropriation.

"I do not think Maj. should be asked to do this without being compensated for his time, and I believe that if you would take this up with the Gov. he would be glad to do this, for it would be a shame to quit when I fully believe that if we can get the information that Maj. sure that he can get from this Man in N.M. and that is — he knows the Man that drove the Car the night that Holmes was killed for the Man, or Men, that did the killing.

"We are all going to get the Skidds [*sic*] about the first of July, by that time the adminestration [*sic*] is going to change here, and we are all going to have to go, and I am so anxious to see the Holmes case cleared up and I feel sure that it can be if we will stay right on the job."

In the light of the two indictments already handed down, Mace's letter is quite interesting because of the questions it raises. Wolters, however, did not appear surprised by it. He wrote to Governor Moody on May 27:

> *This appears to be very important, and I hope that can be done which he suggests. I know that Machen is absolutely on the level, and is competent. I also know that he is poor and has already spent more than he can afford in voluntary work of this kind. It would certainly be a wonderful thing if your administration could finish up the Holmes case.*

Who was the man Machen found? Although it has been suggested that Jim Hodges was the driver, Machen's information apparently differed. Neither Wolters nor Governor Moody show what Machen knew in their files, and no records were located to show anyone else had been arrested in the case.

An Associated Press story, dated May 15, 1930, shows that the "case of Sam Jones, charged with murder in the slaying of DA John A. Holmes, has been continued until the next term of court by agreement of attorneys.

"Jim Hodges, Borger boiler-maker, was charged at the same time with the offense."

Once released on bond neither Jones nor Hodges was returned to jail on the murder charge. Hodges was jailed in Stinnett on June 2, 1930, on a drunk charge, but was fined and released on June 3.

The governor's declaration that he would employ the best lawyers he could find and ask that the murderer be given the death penalty made headlines in September, 1929, but seemed somewhat empty in the mid-1930s. Nothing happened! The evidence against Jones and Hodges apparently was strong, but not strong enough to make a solid case for the prosecution. Neither man ever went to trial, and on October 26, 1945, the State of Texas moved to dismiss the murder charge against Jones "because in the opinion of the State's Attorney, the evidence is insufficient to warrant the probability of a conviction."

District Attorney W. L. McConnell filed the motion and Judge Jack Allen, 84th District Court, approved it.

Writing of his experience in Borger, General Wolters said:

> All criminals have not left Borger and Hutchinson County. Since we left, several crimes have been committed including a bank robbery at Stinnett, but the gratifying part of it is that the new sheriff, constable, and police departments have not only made arrests, but in some instances those culprits are already under conviction and sentences . . . Rescued from the grasp of a conscienceless group that at all times composed an organized minority, though burdened with public debts and numerous municipal problems, the least of which are not fiscal, it has become a secure and safe place within which to live. If I may be permitted to indulge in prophecy, then I do prophesy that within the near future citizens of

140

Borger may say with Saul of old, *"I am a citizen of no mean city."*

During the peak of his administration, the ousted Glenn A. Pace, mayor and then "Man of the Hour," also prophesied about the town:

Borger is another Pittsburgh, Pa., in the making, and in a few years we will see a population of 15,000 and invested manufacturing interests running into the millions . . . With the fuel and water found at Borger, there is no influence in the world that can retard her growth or keep her from making the leading manufacturing city in the Southwest.

Neither prophesy is too far off the mark today.

APPENDUM

STATE OF TEXAS
ADJUTANT GENERAL'S DEPARTMENT
AUSTIN

September 28, 1929

SPECIAL ORDERS
NO. 241½.

1. The following named officers and enlisted men of the Texas National Guard are hereby called to active duty, effective September 29, 1929, and directed to proceed on that date from their respective homes to Borger, Texas, for the purpose of carrying out the orders of the Governor and assisting in the enforcement of the laws of Texas:

OFFICERS

Name	Organization	Station
Brig. Gen. Jacob F. Wolters	56th Cav. Brigade,	Houston
Colonel Oscar Roberts,	143d Infantry,	Taylor
Colonel Louis S. Davidson,	124th Cavalry,	Dallas
Major Horace H. Carmichael,	State Staff,	Austin
Major Clarence E. Parker,	112th Cavalry,	Tyler
Major Harry H. Johnson,	124th Cavalry,	Eastland
Capt. Fred W. Edmiston,	56th Cav. Brigade,	Houston
Capt. John W. Naylor,	124th Cavalry,	Fort Worth
Capt. Charles Williams, MC,	112th Cavalry	Mineral Wells
Capt. McCord McIntire,	112th Cavalry,	Dallas
1st Lt. Louis A. Beecherl,	112th Cavalry,	Dallas
2d Lt. Henry L. Philips,	112th Cavalry,	Dallas
2d Lt. George B. Bennett,	124th Cavalry,	Fort Worth
2d Lt. Lucius A. Waymen,	124th Cavalry,	Fort Worth

ENLISTED MEN

Headquarters Troop, 112th Cavalry, Dallas

Mr. Sgt. Allen B. Wallace,
Staff Sgt. Vincent L. Beakey,
Staff Sgt. John E. Welsh,
Staff Sgt. Richard W. Wilkins,
Sgt. Wm. H. Allen,
Sgt. Wm. H. Laird,
Sgt. Jewell A. Weaver,
Cpl. Ernest E. Connor,
Cpl. John A. Niemeyer,
Pvt. 1cl Raymond Fitzpatrick,
Pvt. 1cl Wm. A. Willis,
Pvt. Edward S. Bridges,

Troop A, 112th Cavalry, Dallas

1st Sgt. Walter T. Moore,
Sgt. Ervin J. Brandt,
Sgt. Thos. R. Houghton,
Corp. Korty J. Hooper,
Corp. Bob I. Golden,
Pvt. Oscar O. Fields,
Pvt. Guy F. Smith,
Pvt. John S. Ballowe,
Pvt. Ray B. Parrish,
Pvt. Wm. M. Baldwin,
Pvt. Alfred H. Hopson,
Pvt. Angelo H. Matassa.

Troop B, 112th Cavalry, Dallas

Sgt. James I. Grant,
Sgt. Geo. H. McNally,
Cpl. Lewis B. Cole,
Cpl. Jack H. Facklin,
Cpl. Louis H. Hanks,
Cpl. Charles F. Woods,
Pvt. 1cl Gus W. Bush,
Pvt. 1cl Joe F. Gandolph,
Pvt. 1cl Henry T. Long,
Pvt. 1cl Earl H. Speckman,
Pvt. 1cl Wilton E. Watson,
Pvt. 1cl Albert C. Yeargan.

Troop E, 112th Cavalry, Dallas

Sgt. Gerald W. Hughes,
Cpl. Robert A. White,
Cpl. Geo. W. Truesdale,
Cpl. Edwin H. Schroeder,
Cpl. Conrad Davis,
Cpl. Sam W. Henry,
Pvt. 1cl Charles S. Kiesewetter,
Pvt. 1cl James M. Forrester,
Pvt. 1cl Sterling P. Hill,
Pvt. 1cl Judge K. Fair,
Pvt. 1cl Richard W. Sills,
Pvt. Raymond G. Hardin.

M.D. Detachment, 112th Cavalry, Mineral Wells

1st Sgt. Raymond E. Cohn,
Stagg Sgt. Fred W. Parnell,
Pvt. 1cl Paul Grimes,
Pvt. 1cl Oscar W. Rankin,
Pvt. 1cl James W. Wedekind,

Troop B, 124th Cavalry, Fort Worth

1st Sgt. James A. Swink,
Sgt. Seaburne Y. Adair,
Sgt. Edwin M. Clark,
Cpl. Robert C. Anderson,
Cpl. Donald W. Wood,
Cpl. Minor D. Taylor,
Pvt. 1cl Curtis Bowen,
Pvt. 1cl Prentis E. Ball,
Pvt. 1cl Wilford N. Carter,
Pvt. Edward L. Best,
Pvt. Homer J. Faulkner,
Pvt. Paul E. Haynes,
Pvt. Harry R. Hooser,
Pvt. Marion N. Pope,
Pvt. 1cl Willie C. Driggers

Troop A, 124th Cavalry,
Fort Worth

Sgt. Rowland E. Lewis,
Sgt. Wallace E. Eddings,
Cpl. Preston Tenpenny,
Cpl. Gordon J. Russell,
Pvt. Geo. B. McClellan,
Pvt. Henry A. Barham,
Pvt. Shelby C. Potter,
Pvt. H. R. Stout,

Pvt. Ray B. Presley,
Pvt. Walter E. Lupton,
Pvt. Richard C. Hardy,
Pvt. Otto P. Adams,
Pvt. J. B. Tenpenny,
Pvt. Ned C. Record,
Pvt. John W. Commander,

2. The officers and enlisted men named herein will be entitled to receive while on active duty the pay and allowances of their respective grades as provided by law for officers and enlisted men of the United States Army.

3. When relieved by proper authority they will return to their respective homes.

4. Travel directed is necessary in the military service of the State.

BY ORDER OF THE GOVERNOR:

OFFICIAL:
TAYLOR NICHOLS,
Asst. Adj. Gen.

ROBT. L. ROBERTSON,
THE ADJUTANT GENERAL.

BIBLIOGRAPHY

BOOKS

Clark, James A. and Halbouty, Michel T. *The Last Boom.* Chapter 14, Martial Law and Hot Oil, pp. 167-173. Random House, New York.

Hamer, Frank. *I'm Frank Hamer, The Life of a Texas Peace Officer.* pp. 143-150. The Pemberton Press, Austin and New York, 1968.

Horlacher, James Levi. *A Year in the Oil Fields.* Press of the Kentucky Kernel, Lexington, Kentucky, 1929.

Lee, Henry. *How Dry We Were: Prohibition Revisited.* Prentice-Hall, New Jersey, April 1963.

Moore, Richard R. *West Texas After the Discovery of Oil, a Modern Frontier.* pp. 23-45. The Pemberton Press, Austin and New York, 1971.

Stanley, F. *The Early Days of the Oil Industry in the Texas Panhandle. 1919-1929.* Hess Publishing Co., Borger, Texas. 1973.

Stephens, Robert W. *Lone Wolf, The Story of Texas Ranger Captain M. T. Gonzaullas.* Taylor Publishing Co., Dallas, Texas. 1979.

Sterling, William Warren. *Trails and Trials of a Texas Ranger.* pp. 97-114. University of Oklahoma Press, Norman, Oklahoma 1959.

White, John H. *Borger, Texas.* Texian Press, Waco, Texas. 1973 (a reprint).

Wolters, Jacob F. *Martial Law and Its Administration.* pp. 54-57, 89-119. Gammel's Book Store, Inc., Printers. 1930.

PAMPHLETS:

Jones, John P. (Slim). Borger, The Little Oklahoma, Volume I. Located in the Southwest Collection, Texas Tech University, Lubbock, Texas.

Jones, John P. (Slim). Borger, The Little Oklahoma, Volume II. Located in the Texas State Archives, Austin, Texas.

Jones, John P. (Slim). Ten Years in the Oil Fields. Publishers and date not given.

Stanley F. The Signal Hill Story. Nazareth, Texas. Date not given.

Stanley, F. The Skellytown, Texas Story. Nazareth, Texas, August, 1974.

Stanley F. The Tex Thornton Story. Nazareth, Texas. January 1975.

NEWSPAPERS:

Amarillo Daily Times and Globe News, numerous articles, 1926 through 1930, Amarillo, Texas.

Austin Statesman, front page, Saturday, September 14, 1929, Austin, Texas.

Borger News Herald, numerous articles, 1926-1930, Borger, Texas.

Daily Oklahoman, numerous articles, 1948-1963, Oklahoma City, Oklahoma.

Kansas City Star, September 22, 1929, Kansas City, Missouri.

The Morning Press, Santa Barbara, California. October 17, 1929.

MAGAZINES:

Human Detective Cases, *Born to be Bad,* Duane Malloy, p. 12, January, 1947.

Master Detective, *Ghost Bandits of the Panhandle,* H.H. Murray, former

Chief of Police of Plainview, Texas with A.D. Nunn, February 1948.

Master Detective, *Borger Death*, H.H. Murray as told to A.D. Nunn, Page 30, May 1948.

THESES:

Garner, L.J., History of Hutchinson County, Southern Methodist University, Dallas, Texas, August 1930.

Henderson, Mary, History of Borger, Texas, West Texas State University, Canyon, Texas, August 1937.

Johnson, Joseph Kelly, Borger: A Study of Community and Personal Disorganization in a Texas Oil Town. University of Texas, August 1930.

ARTICLES:

Borger — Oil-Boom Town. Studies in Sociology, Published by the Department of Sociology, Southern Methodist University, Dallas, Texas. Volume IV, Winter, 1939-Summer, 1940, Numbers 1-2.

Borger: The Last of the Oil Field Booms. Lawrence Hagy. Amarillo, Texas. Undated.

Clyde, The Oil Sniffing Dog. Jim M. Foreman, Black Forest, Colorado. Unpublished.

Derricks in the Dawn; Boom Town; Borger As We Saw It. Apparently a three-part series in the *Borger News Herald.* Undated. Author not shown.

Meaner Than a Junkyard Dog. Jim M. Foreman, Black Forest, Colorado. Unpublished.

Oil is King in the Texas Panhandle. Edward B. Garnett. World's Work, December, 1927.

Old Man Texas Tells the Rip-Roarin' Story of Borger. Garth Massingill. The Junior Historian of the Texas State Historical Association, Austin, Texas. January 1941. pp. 5-6.

Three Questions — Three Answers, a Story from the Life of Dr. Charles Newton Gould (1868-1949). Edited by Henry E. Hertner, Chairman, Potter County Historical Survey Committee, 1967. Amarillo, Texas.

MISCELLANEOUS:

The First Jail Book, Hutchinson County, Texas. 1926-1930.

Panhandle-Plains Historical Review, Volume VIII, 1936. Canyon, Texas.

The Eye Opener, May 1957, Volume 36, No. 11. McAlester, Oklahoma.

Borger Tapes. University of Texas Archives, Austin, Texas.

Reports of the Adjutant General of the State of Texas for the Fiscal Years September 1, 1928 to August 31, 1929 and September 1, 1929 to August 31, 1930. Robert L. Robertson, Adjutant General, Camp Mabry, Austin, Texas.

Various records, Texas Department of Corrections, Huntsville, Texas.

Governor Dan Moody Martial Law File, Texas State Archives, Austin, Texas.

Martial Law File, Historical Documents, Adjutant General's Office, Camp Mabry, Austin, Texas.

INDEX

147

148

150